Ebla Tablets:
S·E·C·R·E·T·S·
OF A FORGOTTEN CITY
Dr. Clifford Wilson

GRADUATE THEOLOGICAL LIBRARY 1962

MB
MASTER BOOKS
A DIVISION OF CLP
SAN DIEGO, CALIFORNIA 92115

Y0-BEZ-967

Ebla Tablets: Secrets of a Forgotten City
Third Edition
—Second Printing May, 1981

Copyright © March, 1979

MASTER BOOKS
Division of CLP
P.O. Box 15666
San Diego, CA 92115

Library of Congress Catalog
Card Number 79-50907

ISBN #0-89051-055-5

All rights reserved.
No part of this publication may be reproduced, stored in a retrieval system, or transmitted in any form or by any means—electronic, mechanical, photocopy, recording, or otherwise—without the prior permission of Master Books, with the exception of brief excerpts in magazine articles and/or reviews.

Cataloging in Publication Data
Wilson, Clifford A. 1923-
   Ebla tablets: secrets of a forgotten city. 3d ed., rev. & enl.
   1. Ebla, Syria. 2. Ebla tablets—Relation to the Old Testament. 3. Syria—Antiquities. I. Title. II. Title: Secrets of a forgotten city.
                221.93   79-50907

Printed in the United States of America.

Cover by Marvin Ross

Table of Contents

461136

Foreword

At times great archaeological discoveries are made by accident. One example is the finding of a huge palace and library at Ras Shamra, the ancient Ugarit, situated on the Mediterranean coast of North Syria. A farmer could not dislodge a stone that was in the way of his relatively primitive plough, called friends to help, and before long an archaeological team had come across one of the most important ancient archives ever discovered. Scholars are still considering the great relevance of that discovery of the 1930's to Bible backgrounds.

Now a somewhat similar discovery has led to equally important findings that have great relevance to Bible backgrounds. In the early 1960's a farmer at Tell Mardikh (a Tell is a hill or mound) in Northern Syria also ran his plough against a large stone object, and when it was eventually dug out it proved to be a bin for storing cereal, dating back to about 1800 B.C. That find has been hailed in Biblical archaeology circles as leading to perhaps the greatest find of the century so far as Bible backgrounds are concerned.

The significance of that grain bin was not

widely recognized at first, but one young graduate in Near Eastern Studies from Rome University was excited by the possible association with other finds. His persistence and personal investigations eventually led to his elders taking the site seriously and a team of excavators began work. Between 1964 and 1973 that "young graduate" (Professor Paolo Matthiae) and his team uncovered the remains of a city that dated to between 2000-1600 B.C. In 1968 a male statue was uncovered with a 26-line inscription, dedicated to Ibbit-Lim, son of Ikris-Hepa, King of Ebla. The city was thus identified, and later excavation has confirmed that indentification. It had already been known in tablets, but the extent of the empire of Ebla has been a shock. The implications for ancient history and Bible backgrounds are very great and will be a source of study for years to come.

This book is now in its third edition and has been updated by the inclusion of an appendix containing pertinent new data of interest that has come to light in recent months.

An Explanation

It is reasonable to believe that in years to come many scholarly tomes will be written about Ebla, giving far more detail and analysis than is yet possible.

However, questions are being asked as to the basic nature of the findings, and sensational exaggerations have already appeared. That is unfortunate, and a balanced appraisal is needed. Because of unexpected personal contacts with the principals involved (both the excavator and the translator of the tablets), I am now able to give a reliable estimate of the importance of these major finds.

Some of the material on Genesis Chapters 1 to 11 has already appeared in other books of mine, such as *In the Beginning God* and *That Incredible Book: The Bible*. That material is included in this new publication because of its relevance in an analysis of the Ebla tablets. The approach to Creation and the Flood has been greatly colored by the *Enuma Elish* and *Gilgamesh* Epics, and they are briefly outlined again so that their relevance is seen.

Clifford Wilson
M.A., B.D., Ph.D.
MONASH UNIVERSITY
VICTORIA, AUSTRALIA
January 1977

Introduction

Suddenly many texts on ancient history are out of date. Accepted theories have been put aside, and scholars are wondering just how their own research—and publications!—will be affected. Seemingly established "facts" relating to early civilizations are being re-examined. Man's relationships with his neighbors around the Fertile Crescent are being re-assessed.

Questions are many, but the answers are not always clear. Where *was* the "cradle of civilization"? Was it Sumer, the Biblical Shinar? Or was it Egypt, as the dwellers on the Nile have so ardently claimed? Was it in fact Syria, the land of the Arameans, thus explaining how Abraham's father was "a wandering Aramean"?

These are some of the questions being asked following the partial excavation of Tell Mardikh, the ancient Ebla, some 30 kilometers south of Aleppo in Northern Syria.

To understand why this and other questions are being asked, this book has been written. This book has been put together as a concise analysis of the more important aspects as they relate to the Bible student who is not a professional archaeologist.

Chapter 1
"Startling Clues to the Old Testament"

So ran the headlines of a recent news release in a San Francisco paper. When one sees such headlines, the normal reaction is skepticism (at least with me). Recovered manuscripts that turn out to be forgeries . . . new information about the life of Jesus . . . computer data about the writing of the Pauline Epistles—they come and go, and very often the stories are worth reading only so one can keep abreast of a topic that is sure to be mentioned at question time after a lecture.

However, sometimes the reports are of a different caliber. The amazing Dead Sea Scrolls were released to the world in this generation, and some of the papyrus findings from Egypt have certainly been sensational. Indeed, despite many false claims, the last fifty years have produced an amazing number of findings that have proved to be of tremendous importance in the study of Bible backgrounds. Archaeological and theological scholars are well aware of the significance of the findings from Ur, Mari, Muzi, Boghazkoi, Ras Shamra, and many more ancient sites.

The new findings at Ebla are in that same category, and possibly they are the most significant discovery yet made, so far as they relate to the background of early Bible times. As a result of this excavation, much of early history will necessarily be rewritten. Already textbooks on ancient history are out of date, and the impact on some areas of Biblical knowledge will indeed be startling, just as this chapter heading suggests.

But let us start at the beginning.

WHERE EBLA IS LOCATED ... AND THE WORK BEGINS

Tell Mardikh—the ancient Ebla—is on the main road to Aleppo in Northern Syria, being not quite half way between Hamath and Aleppo. It is nearer to Aleppo than to Hamath. There is a mound and a small village about one kilometer off the highway. Professor Paolo Matthiae of the Rome University has been excavating there since 1964, but his work was not spectacular until 1968 when his team produced a

statue dedicated to the goddess Ashtar and bearing the name of Ibbit-Lim, a king of Ebla. This endorsed the positive identification of the city. The kingdom of Ebla had previously been known in Sumerian, Akkadian, and Egyptian texts, and the excavators had good clues when they began digging in this 50-feet high mound. Now their hopes were bright for the future.

Encouraged by the statue finding, the work continued, and in 1974 patience was rewarded by the finding of 42 tablets in a cuneiform script. That sort of find is "better than gold" for an archaeologist, but that was only the beginning. In the 1975 season some 15,000 tablets were recovered. To bring the report up to date, the excavators recently reported (with a smile!) that 1976 was a poor season—only 1,600 tablets were found!

Professor Giovanni Pettinato, also of the University of Rome, is the epigrapher working on the tablets, and some of what follows stems from his reports, both in the *Biblical Archaeologist* of May, 1976, and in public lectures and discussions at the University of Michigan in November, 1976. Professor Matthiae also lectured at that time, and both Professors were most cooperative in two days of lectures, discussion, and question and answer sessions. It was my privilege to participate in these public functions, as well as in more private meetings with the archaeologists and with a number of leaders in the field of Biblical archaeology and Semitic studies.

Professor David Noel Freedman of the University of Michigan also participated in depth: it was he who traveled to Rome especially to investigate these sensational new findings, and his report was written up in *TIME Magazine* of October 18, 1976. Professor Freedman is highly regarded in archaeological circles. He is Editor of *New Perspectives in Biblical Archaeology* and Editor of the prestigious quarterly journal *Biblical Archaeologist*.

In introducing Professor Matthiae at the commencement of the public lectures mentioned above, Professor Freedman stated that these findings were of major significance for Near Eastern studies, for Biblical studies, and for the study of the origins of civilization and culture. He went on to say that "The New Cambridge History" has suddenly become "The Old Cambridge History". In fact, so significant are these new findings at Ebla that suddenly all the standard textbooks dealing with the history of the Near East are out of date.

WHAT THE EXCAVATORS FOUND

Only a small part of the palace itself has yet been excavated, and this includes a large area which appears to have been an audience court with two porticoes. It was

Tablets from the ancient city of Ebla discovered at the Tell Mardikh.   Religious News Service Photo.

apparently used as a place of reception. There was an imposing facade for the palace, and there were two entrances. At the center of one entrance was a monumental doorway. There was a beautiful stairway going up from this monumental doorway, and there was also a large court.

Behind the portico were three rooms, and it was here that the excavators found the subsidiary library, with its 15,000 clay tablets. We say "subsidiary" because it was not the main library of the palace itself. When the palace proper is excavated it is hoped that the major collection will come to light, with untold possibilities for increasing our knowledge of ancient times and early Bible backgrounds.

In another room, which was apparently a store room, the excavators found another 1,000 tablets, this apparently being the room of the scribes. Writing implements were found.

In another room they found 800 tablets that were basically dealing with administration.

In addition to the tablets, there were beautiful carved wooden figures found in these rooms, and there were other delightful artistic treasures. One of the beautifully carved figures was of a royal female, holding what appears to be a scepter. There were also a number of seal impressions and another figure of a female deity.

Among the findings were composite

plaques in wood, gold, and lapis lazulae. Plaster covered some of the plaques, and one sheet of gold was also found. Most of the gold had already been taken, presumably by the palace destroyers.

One text stated that the city had a population of 260,000 and it was divided into two sections. These were the acropolis and the lower city. Various servants and officials of the city are listed.

THE LINKS WITH SARGON THE GREAT AND NARAM-SIN

There are a number of historical texts which can be tied in with other known records, such as those of the city of Mari, coming down to the time of Naram-Sin who eventually defeated the Eblahites so decisively. It appears that the city was defended by mercenaries rather than by its own army. Professor Pettinato conjectures that this is probably the reason why Akkad finally prevailed over Ebla.

The tablets would appear to date to the two last generations of the city, somewhere about 2,300 B.C.—possibly 100 years earlier. The final destruction was about 2250 B.C.

Naram-Sin was himself the grandson of the great Sargon of Akkad. Possibly Sargon's victory against the city, at an earlier time, was not as complete as that of Naram-Sin, for Naram-Sin not only conquered the city but also claims to have subjugated it in a way nobody before him had done. Despite his boastful claim, the details are not yet entirely clear at this point of time.

A Sargon is mentioned in the tablets but it is not specifically stated that it is Sargon of Akkad. It is possible that the city was destroyed by Naram-Sin some time after the city had been captured by Sargon. The relationship between them (Naram-Sin and Sargon) is a point of conjecture: at the time of this writing, the two Italian Professors differ as to whether Sargon or Naram-Sin had destroyed the city. This means that there is still debate as to whether the earliest date for this level of Ebla is 2,400 B.C. or 2,300 B.C. These are questions that are not likely to be resolved until more scholarly work has been done on the tablets.

The findings at Ebla will be analyzed in great detail, but it will not be done in a day, or a week, or a month, or even a year. Even if no more tablets are recovered, those 17,-000 already on hand ensure the attention of scholars for years to come. A generation has passed and we are still talking and writing about the Nuzi, the Mari, and the Ras Shamra tablets. Those from Ebla are every bit as important and will demand as much if not more attention.

THE WORK HAS ONLY
JUST BEGUN

There has been no more than a scratching of the surface (not literally!) with the information yet given to the public. Thousands of the tablets have not yet been translated, and at the time of this writing there are thousands that have not even been categorized, let alone translated.

This being the case, it is a reasonable question to ask if there should be analyses of the findings put out at this early stage. To answer that question, it is reasonable to ask another. Should Professor David Noel Freedman, a world-renowned figure in Biblical archaeology, have made a special visit to Rome to interview the Italian archaeologists? We are grateful that he did and that his conference was followed by a guarded report, first to the scholarly world of Biblical archaeology and then to the world at large. The answer is of course he should have done all that, and he is owed a debt of gratitude.

Knowledge cannot be indefinitely hidden, even though there might be legitimate reasons for withholding it for a time. With archaeology sometimes it is desirable to hide such knowledge, if only to keep unwelcome amateurs away from the site. There are already too many legitimate tablets on the black markets of the world.

At one time it was also thought that the

findings might be the cause of further tension between the governments of Syria and Israel, but this is unlikely. The Israelis are always interested in whatever touches their own long history, and the Syrians are pleased to find that they can put in a legitimate claim to be the original "cradle of civilization". To think that their history can be traced back to a civilization rivaling that of Sumer and Egypt is something over which to rejoice. Syrians can raise their heads high, with the knowledge that very possibly many of the forefathers of the Hebrew people came from their territory.

The findings at Ebla undoubtedly mean a turning point in the history of the ancient Near East. Modern-day Syria shares the pride and the excitement of the new discoveries.

In the following pages we shall see how these discoveries demand a new place for this ancient kingdom, centering out from the territory of modern Syria. We shall also see that the chapter heading, "Startling Clues to the Old Testament", is justified.

Chapter 2
What the Tablets
Are All About

It is probable that the 17,000 tablets so far recovered are not from the major royal archives, but are rather a collection of records that were kept near the central court. Here the provisions were stored, tribute was collected, and apprentice scribes did their copying from tablets which they would take temporarily from the royal archives themselves. A wide variety of tablets were copied, and this is of tremendous importance, for it means that today we have a wide range of these copied tablets available for study.

The two rooms where the main body of 15,000 tablets were recovered were close to the entrance to the palace. If the royal archives themselves are found as excavation proceeds, the potential for the study of

Bible backgrounds and ancient history is tremendous.

Many of the tablets found were exceptionally large, being 40 cms long, 50 columns wide, and having up to 3,000 lines on a single tablet.

As Professor Pettinato has pointed out, these are the sorts of tablets that scholars dream about but rarely find. Personal names are included, and in one text alone 260 geographic names have been given. Other texts give lists of animals, fish, birds, professions, and names of officials.

There are literary texts with mythological backgrounds, incantations, collections of proverbs, and hymns to various deities. Rituals associated with the gods are mentioned, many of these gods being known in Babylonian literature of a later period. These include Enki, Enlil, Utu, Inana, Tiamut, Marduk, and Nadu. The god of the city of Kish is also mentioned.

One of the ceremonies described is that of the anointing of the king, and this seems to have some similarity to the later practice in the Old Testament. Apparently the king was elected and was recognized as being the person who had power at that time. Details of this are somewhat obscure, and we await further light in this area.

Sacrificial systems are mentioned, and once again it is interesting to realize that the old arguments against the Hebrew sacrificial system being quite unknown at the time of the Conquest are shown to be fallacious. Offerings of various kinds were being made at the time when this King Ebrum ruled, somewhere before 2250 B.C.

TARIFFS, TRIBUTES, AND TREATIES

Most of the tablets deal with economic matters, tariffs, receipts, and other commercial dealings. We shall see, however, that they also dealt with other matters, such as offerings to the gods.

The commercial tablets prescribed what tariffs should be set and what tribute should be paid. There are contracts of sale and documents about the possession of goods. They deal with shipping and bills of lading and refer to unfinished supplies that have been brought into the city. Payment is mentioned in terms of silver and gold—the ratio of gold to silver varied somewhat, but it was around 5,6, or 7 to 1. Ebla was the center of a great trading empire, with trade relations stretching right across the Fertile Crescent, with the possible exception of Egypt. As far as is yet known, there was no direct trade contact with that country.

This city was in contact with other cities all over the Near East. One of the interesting illustrations of this comes from the list of rations given to messengers as they traversed certain routes, with the names of the cities given. There are lists of towns in their geographic regions and even lists of the towns that are subject to Ebla. Biblical towns of later times are included, such as Ashdod and Sidon.

There are also lists of rations for palace personnel, and there are dating points within the tablets themselves, making it possible at least to be sure of the general period. In archaeological terms, it is Early Bronze IV (E.B.IV). There are royal ordinances and edicts, letters of state, and records of significant treaties made between Ebla and other places and peoples.

One of the treaties is between the city of Ebla and Asshur, one of the chief cities of the Assyrians at a later time, but also the name of the Assyrian people as such. The origin of the name Asshur itself is found in the Table of Nations, at Genesis chapter 10. We learn there that it was he who built Nineveh, and Asshur itself rivaled Nineveh as one of the great Assyrian cities of antiquity. It was relatively common for a great man to give his name to a city he founded. The treaty at Ebla was with the king of the Assyrians.

VOCABULARY LISTS
IN TWO LANGUAGES

There are syllabaries of grammatical texts, making it possible to go from one language to another. There are no less than

114 Sumerian Eblahite vocabularies, these being the first such lists recovered from any ancient site. One of these vocabulary tablets contains nearly 1,000 translated words, and it has 18 duplicates.

It has long been known that scribes in Assyria copied tablets from Babylonia, but it is now established that scholars in Mesopotamia had also copied some of their tablets from the Syrian libraries.

When the first tablets were found, it was soon realized that this city used a very ancient language of the North West Semitic group which was previously unknown. Professor Pettinato labeled this "Paleo-Canaanite". In layman's terms, this means "ancient Canaanite". At the close of his article in *Biblical Archaeologist* Professor Pettinato tells us,

> "The pronominal and verbal systems, in particular, are so clearly defined that one can properly speak of a Paleo-Canaanite language closely akin to Hebrew and Phoenician."

These Ebla tablets are written in a Sumerian script, with Sumerian logograms adapted to represent Akkadian words and syllables. About 1,000 words were recovered initially (hundreds more later) in vocabulary lists. The words are written out in both Sumerian logograms and Eblaic syllabic-type writing. These offered an invaluable key to the interpretation of many of the Ebla texts.

Logograms represent root meaning and do not have grammatical indications, whereas with syllabic writings the words themselves are spelled out phonetically. At Ebla the Sumerian texts were written in logograms, and the syllabic writing was put down in the dialect of Ebla.

Logograms were also used for Eblaic itself, and in those cases the meaning was the same whether the word was in Sumerian or in Eblaic. The bilingual vocabulary made it possible to check out which was the actual wording used. There was no mixture of Sumerian and Eblaic in the actual text: Sumerian texts were all Sumerian and the Eblaic texts were all Eblaic, but Sumerian logograms were used in them and could be interpreted by scholars as though they were in a Semitic language.

It is important to notice that the tablets indicate that there was considerable bilingualism, at least with the scholars. About 80% of the tablets were Sumerian and 20% Paleo-Canaanite. It appears that when the tablets were written in Sumerian, they were read as though they were North West Semitic. In this, there is some similarity to the writing and reading of Chinese scripts today in that one common script would be pronounced differently in various parts of China. A man living in Canton might not understand the speech of the man in Peking, but they could communicate by writing.

Another over-simplistic explanation is linked to numerals. The figure "3" calls for a different word when it is pronounced, according to whether the reader is English, French, or German. The "trois" of the Frenchman is different from the "three" of the Englishman, but it is not difficult to accept that there was a common root. We see an elaboration of that with the Sumerian symbols sometimes used by the scribes of Ebla.

The vocabularies at Ebla were distinctively Semitic: the word "to write" is k-t-b (as in Hebrew), while that for "king" is "malikum", and that for "man" is "adamu". The closeness to Hebrew is surprising.

Undoubtedly the new tablets will throw tremendous light on pronunciations and on some literary forms in the Old Testament. It is also true that the Old Testament itself will be of tremendous value as these texts continue to be studied and their meanings examined. There will be inter-relationship, for the Old Testament will throw light on the tablets from Ebla, and as the tablets themselves are understood it is probable that there will also be a great amount of light thrown on the early Old Testament records. There will probably be a great amount of knowledge gained from the study of the religious practices in the background of these early people; it will be interesting to compare them with the inspired Bible records.

Professor Pettinato makes the point that the Ebla lists are the oldest vocabularies recorded in history, being 500 years earlier than any previously known. The documents were prepared by a very efficient school of scribes. No longer can it be argued that early culture must necessarily be linked with Mesopotamia at such sites as Uruk, Fara, Nippur, and others. Many of the tablets found at Ebla are actually identical with some of those from the Mesopotamian sites of Fara and Abu Salabikh. No less than 50 tablets from Ebla have been identified as being also at those two Sumerian centers. It is true that there was Sumerian influence on the tablets at Ebla, but this was two-way traffic.

By way of summary it can be said that linguistically we are very fortunate to have this vocabulary, which by 1976 had given a word-list of approximately 2,500 words. This can be compared with Ugaritic, where there are about 2,000 words. However, the Ebla vocabulary is more extensive in giving place names and also the names of people. As we have said above, there are now 114 separate tablets recovered that are bilingual dictionaries. In all these, Semitic and Sumerian equivalents are given, and this means that if the present-day scholar knows one of those languages, he can interpret the other.

TABLETS DEALING WITH JUDICIAL PROCEEDINGS

It is relevant to note that some of the tablets deal with judicial proceedings. There are elaborations as to the penalties incurred when a person is injured, and there are details about various trials. Some of these points make foolish the former criticisms against the possibility of the existence of a Mosaic law-code. Here is a civilization about 1,000 years earlier than that of Moses, and in writing it gives all sorts of details about the administration of justice. It is clearly a highly developed civilization, with concepts of justice and individual rights to the fore. To suggest that Moses could not have dealt with such cases is ludicrous.

Two tablets deal with case law, and the law code of Ebla must now be recognized as the oldest ever yet found. In dealing with the penalties for injuries, distinction is made according to the nature of the act. An injury caused by the blow of a hand merited a different penalty from one caused by a weapon such as a dagger. Differing penalties are prescribed for various offenses.

There is elaborate discussion of case law, with varying conditions recognized for what at first look might seem to be the same crime. In the case of a complaint involving sexual relations, if the girl was able to prove that she was a virgin and that the act was forced on her, the penalty against the man was death. Otherwise he would pay a fine that varied according to circumstances.

Once again we have written documents that point to law codes hundreds of years before Moses. These are the oldest substantial fragments pointing to such a law code yet recovered. This thriving civilization at Ebla is about 1,000 years before Moses. Arguments of a generation ago that Moses' law code was too early for his time, and that his writing must therefore be attributed to the later prophets, are clearly erroneous.

The Ebla laws dealing with sex offenses are remarkably close to those found in Deuteronomy 22:22-30. In that passage there is a distinction made according to whether the girl was a virgin and cried out for help, or was a willing participant in the act. This is very close to the law at Ebla.

THE GENUINENESS
OF THE FINDS

There is no question as to the authenticity of this remarkable find. The sheer numbers of tablets are overwhelming, and any thought of "salting" the dig is ludicrous. Falsification is out of the question. In any case, the linguistic pattern is very complex, and it would be absurd to think of

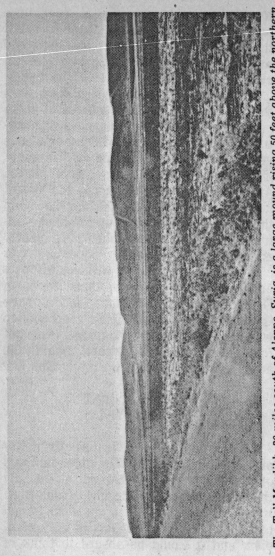

The Tell Mardikh, 30 miles south of Aleppo, Syria, is a large mound rising 50 feet above the northern Syrian plain. It covers the intriguing buried civilizations of the ancient city of Ebla.
Photo courtesy of Robert Durnal.

forgers undertaking a work of such proportions. There is authenticity as to the historical facts, for they can be tied in with other areas, with known dates and locales. In addition, of course, they have been found by competent scholars at the right place, where they had correctly anticipated that artifacts would be located. The conditions of discovery were properly controlled by qualified scholars, and the records were found in the precincts of a great royal palace that has begun to be uncovered—the sort of area where such a discovery might logically be expected.

Posterity can be grateful for the way the tablets have been preserved. When the walls collapsed, they protected the records. Many of them remained on the fallen shelves still housing them, though large numbers had fallen on the floor alongside the shelves.

Professor Freedman made an interesting observation in his public lecture at Michigan. In the past 100 years the Holy Land has been the most excavated area of the whole world. It would be a reasonable estimate to suggest that in all the years of excavation at Holy Land sites, at all the levels of all the cities excavated, the total number of tablets found would about equal the total number of tablets found in one season (1975) at this one site (Ebla), at only one level.

It can be put in another way. About 17,000

tablets and significant fragments have been found at this site, and they date to approximately 2,400 B.C. to 2,250 B.C. This would be about four times the grand total of all the tablets found, dating to that period, from all other sites. The nearest in magnitude for the number of tablets would be Mari, dating several hundred years later.

Chapter 3
Personal Names
and Places
in the Tablets

A number of personal names in the Ebla documents are very similar to names used at later times in the Old Testament. One such name is Michael (mi-ka-ilu) which means, "Who is like El?" A related form, also in the Ebla Texts, is *mi-ka-ya* which is well-known in the Bible, with the *ya* ending replacing the *el*. Other names are ab-ra-mu (Abram/Abraham), is-ra-ilu (Israel), e-sa-um (Esau), da-'u-dum (David), sha-'u'-lum (Saul), and Ish-ma-Il (Ishmael) which means "Il (El-God) has heard me."

Other examples given by Professor Pettinato are En-na-ni-Il which gave over to En-na-ni-Ya, Il/Ya has mercy on me; A-dam-Ma-lik, man of Malik; 'il-ha-il, Il is strength; Eb-du-Ra-sa-ap, Servant of

Rasaph; Ish-a-bu, A man is the father; Ish-i-lum, A man is the god; I-sa-Ya, Ya has gone forth; I-ad-Da-mu, The hand of Damu; and Ib-na-Ma-lik, Malik has created. Hebrew scholars recognize remarkable similarities to later Hebrew in the Old Testament, and Professor Pettinato himself states, in the *Biblical Archaeologist* mentioned before, "Many of these names occur in the same form in the Old Testament, so that a certain interdependence between the culture of Ebla and that of the Old Testament must be granted."

HEBREW WORDS AKIN TO EBLA WORDS

At Ebla, the king has the Sumerian title "en", and according to the vocabulary lists already described, the Paleo-Canaanite equivalent is "Malek". This is virtually the same as the Hebrew word for "king" in the Old Testament, "melek". The elders of the kingdom were the "abbu", remarkably close to "abba" (father) of the Old Testament. At very many points the similarity to Old Testament Hebrew is very close.

Man's search for the true God and for spiritual truth is shown by many of the personal names at Ebla. "Mi-ka-Ya", meaning "Who is like Ya?" replaced "Mi-ka-Il", meaning "Who is like Il (El)?" "En-na-ni-Ya" meant, "Ya has mercy on me." "Re-i-na-Adad", telling the world that "Adad (a god) is our shepherd", reminds the Christian of Psalm 23 where the ultimate of that searching for divine leading and protection is found as the psalmist exclaims, *"The Lord is my shepherd."*

Professor Pettinato discusses the names of some of the gods attested at Ebla, including "IL/EL of the Ugaritic texts", and tells us ". . . from Ebrum on, Il was substituted for by Ya. . . . It appears evident that under Ebrum a new development in West Semitic religious concepts took place that permitted the rise of Ya". Dagan of the Old Testament is well-known, being associated with several places already known to scholars, including "Dagan of Canaan". This indicates that the term "Canaan" was known much earlier than previously believed.

He also makes the point that Ashtar was a masculine god at Ebla, "unlike his Mesopotamian counterpart Ashtarte". Ashtarte (or Ashtaroth, another translation) was a female deity, well-known to the Israelites in the days of the Conquest of Canaan. It is interesting to notice in passing that in modern U.F.O. literature there is a considerable amount of contact with a "Mr. Ashtar", apparently propagating the claims of a false Messiah.

OLD TESTAMENT CITIES
REFERRED TO, INCLUDING
SODOM AND GOMORRAH.

One aspect of special interest to Bible students is that a number of Old Testament cities are mentioned. There are cities that were previously known in 1st and 2nd Millennium records, but now they are referred to in these 3rd Millennium B.C. tablets. There is Salim (possibly the city of Melchizedec), Hazor, Lachish, Megiddo, Gaza, Dor, Sinai, Ashtaroth, and Joppa. Of special interest is Urusalima (Jerusalem) this being the earliest known reference to this city.

Although a city called Salim is referred to in the tablets, there is no indication as to its geographic locations. It is referred to separately from Urusalima (Jerusalem), and this would indicate that the two cities are separate.

Two of the towns mentioned are Sodom and Gomorrah. Here we are transported back to about 2,300 B.C., and we find that these towns were regularly visited, being on the route of the King's Highway that ran down from Damascus.

That is not all. There are actually five "cities of the Plain" (to use the Biblical term at Genesis 14:2), and these were Sodom, Gomorrah, Admah, Zeboiim, and Zoar. We are told in that same verse that an earlier name for Zoar was Bela. These tablets from Ebla refer very precisely, by name, to those five cities of the plain, and at this point we quote from Professor Freedman's public address in November, 1976.

> "This record precedes the great catastrophe which many scholars, especially of more recent vintage, have regarded as entirely fictional."

He goes on to say that many scholars had regarded the Biblical story of the destruction of Sodom and Gomorrah as an etiological [seeking to assign a cause] tale, set down to explain the collapse of those cities, but now from Ebla we are taken to the other side of the catastrophe. We find that these were real cities, cities that were flourishing at the time of these tablets.

Damascus is mentioned a number of times This is very interesting, for this means that this city has been in continuous existence from approximately 2,300 BC. and perhaps even considerably earlier.

THE RELIABILITY OF
THE BIBLICAL TEXT

Another of the towns referred to is Carchemish, and Professor Pettinato made the point that the prophet Isaiah has a remarkable knowledge of this name, as shown in the text preserved at Isaiah 10:9. This preserves the ancient name of the god

"Chemosh", the Moabite god known in later Bible times.

At one point in the discussion about the names of the gods, Professor Pettinato comments, "One may again marvel at the reliability of the Biblical text" (as to the preservation of the name Kemish). He further states, "This suggests that the Massoretes had very ancient documents at their disposal." It was the Massoretes who introduced vowel signs into Hebrew, long after Old Testament times.

The "reliability of the Biblical text" to which the Professor referred, relates to Isaiah 10:9, where the prophet refers to "Carchemish" by its old name—"Car" (Kar) is "town", and so he was referring to "the town (or city) of Chemish."

In a passing comment Professor Pettinato stated that this indicated that Isaiah obviously had access to very old source material.

We have seen that the name "Canaan" is also mentioned in the tablets, and this indicates that the name is much older than many scholars had previously thought. As this word "Canaan" is actually used in the texts, this precludes the possibility of the term "Paleo-Canaanite" being branded as anachronistic. Pettinato himself states that there are so many correlations with 1st and 2nd Millennium Canaanite terms, that the description "Paleo-Canaanite" is fully justified (p. 50 B.A. article).

This sign on the road from Aleppo directs traffic to the activities at the Tell Mardikh.

Photo courtesy of Robert Durnal.

DILMUN AND THE
GARDEN OF EDEN?

It is interesting also to know that the place Dilmun is referred to as a geographic site, and this is of special interest because of a tablet about Dilmun, already known to archaeologists. This is in the *Epic of Emmerkar* which has been accepted as an embellishment of the Garden of Eden story. Dilmun is now seen to be an actual site, known in ancient times.

S. H. Hooke quotes as follows (*Middle Eastern Mythology*, p.114) from the Sumerian *Epic of Emmerkar:*

"The land Dilmun is a pure place,
  the land Dilmun is a clean place,
The land Dilmun is a clean place,
  the land Dilmun is a bright place.
In Dilmun the raven uttered no cry,
The kite uttered not the cry of the kite,
The lion killed not,
The wolf snatched not the lamb,
Unknown was the kid-killing dog,
Unknown was the grain-devouring boar . . .
The sick-eyed says not "I am sick-headed,"
Its [Dilmun's] old woman says not
     "I am an old woman,"
Its old man says not "I am an old man,"
Unbathed is the maid, no sparkling water
     is poured in the city,
Who crosses the river [of death?]
     utters no . . .
The wailing priests walk not about him,

The singer utters no wail,
By the side of the city he utters
      no lament.''

For the Christian, much of this is seen in its ideal in the new Jerusalem. The lion lies down with the lamb. There is no more weeping, and all tears are wiped away. The blessings of Eden are restored, and much more besides. The ancient world grasped after such a golden age, but its perfection is seen in the pages of the Bible, God's revelation to man.

My major point at the moment is that Dilmun is known in the Ebla tablets as an actual site in antiquity—a point of real interest to Bible students.

THE EXTENT OF THE EBLA EMPIRE

The trading activities of the city were very great. In fact, all the Biblical towns listed above occur a number of times in the tablets so far translated. It is clear that Ebla played a highly significant role in the political, economic, and cultural history of the entire Near East in the 3rd Millennium B.C. In fact, it is now established that this Syrian Empire was as large in extent as that of the great Sargon of Akkad.

Before the finding of these tablets it was widely believed that Syria and Palestine were at best sparsely populated in these times, or were probably occupied by nomadic tribes. Now it has been shown that there were many city-states, each having its own king, and they were often in close contact with each other. It seems that Ebla itself was the most important of these cities, and that a number of smaller principalities revolved around the city.

Apparently Ebla headed up the most powerful center in the whole of the Near East in the third millennium B.C. To the south its influence reached to Sinai and included Israel, Lebanon, and Syria as we know them today. Its power extended to Cyprus in the west, while to the north it extended to Karmish (Carchemish), and possibly also to Hattu. Toward the east, its power extended to the highlands of Mesopotamia.

THE PROBLEM OF UR— NORTH OR SOUTH?

No doubt there will be some problems for conservative scholars as well as for "liberals", as a result of the finding of these tablets. One has already come to light, in that a city of Ur is referred to in the trade tablets. It is described as being "in the territory of Haran".

As a conservative, I confess that at first I personally was somewhat disappointed. I am the producer of a number of audio-visuals on Bible backgrounds, and one of them is based on Sir Leonard Woolley's findings at the city of Ur. When it was first stated that Ur was "in the territory of Haran", it seemed likely that the city excavated by Woolley was not Abraham's city after all. That excavation produced many evidences of remarkable culture, and some of them were of direct relevance in the study of Bible backgrounds. Some of the tablets actually coincided with Abraham's period, though he himself was not personally mentioned.

Actually many of Woolley's findings as to culture are of great relevance to the background of Abraham, whether the city was Ur of Abraham or not. Trade links ensure the exchange of cultural patterns, and gold vessels, musical instruments, and religious rituals from Ur are important in showing those patterns.

However, second thoughts led to the realization that Woolley's city of Ur was probably Abraham's city of Ur also. It is a common feature around the world for there to be cities with the same names. I was born in Concord, New South Wales, Australia, but on my visits to the United States I quite often stay with a pastor, a close personal friend, in Concord, California. They are different cities of course! So it has been through the centuries. Woolley's city WAS Ur, and so is the northern city named in the Ebla tablets as being "in the territory of Haran".

So I asked myself, "Which WAS

Abraham's city?" Haran also is identified with Abraham, in that he went from Ur to Haran in the north, and he stayed there until his father died. At first sight this would suggest that THIS was the Biblical city of Ur, but there is other evidence that must be considered.

The city that Woolley excavated was called Ur, for this was established by tablet findings, including one record about Ur-Nammu, a king of Ur just before Abraham's time. It is relevant to notice that the Bible actually delineates which Ur it was, for it specifically refers to "Ur of the Chaldees." This is made very clear as soon as we are introduced to Abraham: his birth is recorded in Genesis 11:27, and in the very next verse we read that Abraham's brother died in the land of his nativity, "in Ur of the Chaldees." Verse 31 of the same chapter tells how they went forth from Ur of the Chaldees to go into the land of Canaan, and that they came to Haran and dwelt there. If this was merely a journey from "Ur in the territory of Haran" to Haran itself, it would hardly merit the Biblical explanation which clearly demands a journey of some moment, to another land.

At Acts chapter 7 verse 2 we read that God appeared to Abraham "when he was in Mesopotamia before he dwelt in Haran." The fourth verse of that chapter also states that Abraham came out of the land of the

Chaldeans, and for some time dwelt in Haran.

"UR OF THE CHALDEES": NEW SIGNIFICANCE

It is accepted by scholars that the use of the term "of the Chaldees" (presumably by a later editor) is deliberate, indicating that the Mesopotamian Ur is referred to. In other words, this legitimate editing note is saying that it was the southern city of Ur that was the home base of the patriarch Abraham. If the writer knew of two cities of Ur, obviously it would be desirable to delineate one, and the Bible writer has done just that. This editing note now takes on a new significance in view of the tablet from Ebla. The geographical editing note suggests that the Bible writer knew there was another city that could be confused with the Biblical city of the same name. Thus the writer is making it abundantly clear that it is the southern city to which he is referring, the one near the Persian Gulf in ancient times.

The fact of a northern city of Ur has been known to scholars for a considerable period of time, and there has been extended debate as to whether the Biblical city would be the southern or the northern one. However, nobody knew just where the northern city really was, though its existence was confirmed by recovered tablets. Now that we know the northern city is "in the territory of Haran," it becomes clear that this is NOT the Biblical city. Abraham's center was in southern Mesopotamia, and by implication the Ebla tablets have actually cleared up a problem at this point, in favor of the "Woolley" city. The editing note in the Bible turns out to be a necessary and even remarkable piece of local color.

Thus one of the side-products of the new Ebla excavation has been to clear up a difficulty. What seemed to be a problem turns out to contain within it the solution to another problem. Sir Leonard Woolley's claim that he excavated Abraham's city has been strengthened.

This does not preclude the possibility of Ebla's King Ebrum having ethnic ties with Abraham or with Abraham's people who became known as the Hebrews. As we study the Bible records it becomes clear that Abraham's descendants had cultural contacts with the people in the general area around Ebla, such as when Jacob married two daughters of Laban. Laban lived in the general area of that northern culture.

We also find outside the Bible that Ur near the Persian Gulf had cultural ties with these northern people. The people of both cities worshipped the moon god Nannar, and there were trade relations between the peoples of the north and the south.

Chapter 4
Records
of Creation

After Professor Pettinato's public lecture, he was asked a great number of questions by those whose theological standpoint ranged from "fundamentalist" to "liberal". Much of it was put on tape with cassettes, and this of course meant that his answers were from that point public property. The Professor was asked if it was true that there were Creation and Flood tablets similar to those in the Bible. This was a matter where considerable interest was shown, for there had been some conflict in the press reports. One report had stated that there were such tablets, but another had claimed that this was not according to fact. As only Professor Pettinato was qualified to give a definite answer, it is not surprising that he was questioned so closely.

The questions about the Flood produced a fairly routine answer—that there was a record of flood that lasted for seven days, and it was rather similar to that of the Babylonian version in the *Epic of Gilgamesh*.

A NEW CREATION TABLET

The questions about the Creation story were more persistent, and the Professor acknowledged that there was such a tablet. He stated that the record appeared to be remarkably like that found in the first verses of Genesis—"In the beginning, God created the heavens and the earth." Pressed as to what the tablet actually stated, he said that the creation tablet was closer to Genesis Chapter 1 than anything yet discovered. It said that there was a time when there was no heaven, and Lugal ("the great one"), formed it out of nothing; there was no earth, and Lugal made it; there was no light, and he made it. It must be stressed that the Professor was talking in answer to questions, and was not giving an exact translation.

Professor Pettinato went on to say that this was a ten-line poem, beautifully inscribed, but that there were parts of it that he had not yet been able to translate. There were three copies of the poem. He elaborated that the "light" was associated with the sun and the moon, and that the concept of creation was to make something out of nothing. The word "Lugal" originally meant "the great one", and it came to mean "king".

This tablet is dramatically different from other records such as the Babylonian *Enuma Elish* and the *Epic of Atrahasis* which have such grotesque absurdities as gods fighting, cutting each other in half, making the earth from one half of a monster goddess and the heaven from the other, with the Tigris River flowing from one eye and the Euphrates from the other.

A FIRST-MILLENNIUM ORAL HEBREW TRADITION IN A THIRD-MILLENNIUM WRITTEN DOCUMENT

When this close similarity to Genesis Chapter 1 was first mentioned to a group of scholars present at that time, there was a stunned silence. Then one of them—who shall remain nameless—made the comment, "A first-millennium oral Hebrew tradition, in a third-millennium written document?"

That was not the time or the place for that to be elaborated, but every one of the scholars in that rather "high-powered" group knew that there were far-reaching implications of this new finding. One such implication related to the dating of other written records of the creation narrative: I shall explain this, and then point out the relevance to the Bible record.

ANCIENT BABYLONIAN RECORDS

The *Epic of Gilgamesh* and the *Enuma Elish* were found in the palace of the Assyrian King Ashurbanipal who died about 627 B.C. He sent scribes out over the then known world, to recover tablets dealing with ancient times. They went to palaces and temples and brought back many thousands of originals and copies to Ashurbanipal's palace. It could be claimed that he was the first serious archaeologist.

The Babylonian account was written on seven tablets averaging about 150 lines each, and about nine-tenths of the epic can be reconstructed. The seven tablets possibly have some relationship to the seven days of creation referred to in the Bible story. Similarly, in the Babylonian tablets we are told of the creation of man on the sixth tablet, and some scholars see a similarity to the Bible story of creation where man is created on the sixth day. It was first brought to the notice of Bible students in 1876 when the Assyriologist George Smith published his translation of what he called "The Chaldean Account of Genesis." As we said above, Ashurbanipal's Assyrian version was based on the earlier Babylonian epic.

In this Babylonian account of creation there are gods fighting, and there is a crude polytheism (a presentation of many gods) which is simply missing from the Bible's majestic account of the Triune God in His work of creation.

Another Babylonian story of creation was the Babylonian *Epic of Atrahasis*. Until 1965 only about one-fifth of this was known, but now about four-fifths of this epic have been restored. This particular version dates to about 1630 B.C. and fragmentary copies of it also were found in the Assyrian libraries of Nineveh, dating to about one thousand years later. Other fragments have been found at Babylon, at Nippur, and at the ancient Hittite capital of Bogazkoy—this last copy dates to about 1000 B.C. (See "Buried History", *Quarterly Journal of The Australian Institute of Archaeology,* September 1968, p. 69)

DIFFERENCES FROM THE BIBLE RECORD

Typical of the differences is the way in which the heavens and the earth were supposed to be created. In the Babylonian account the god Marduk cuts the goddess Tiamat in two before he proceeds to use her mutilated body in the work of creation. The Bible record is very different from these fantastic and grotesque ideas. There we read of God who is all-powerful, the One who created the worlds by the word of His power.

The Babylonian story is addressed to the god Marduk, and this is quite different from the Biblical version in which God reveals the details of creation to man, details that could not otherwise be known.

According to the Babylonian version, after Marduk was successful, the rebel gods feared that he would make them his servants forever. They appealed to him for leniency and gave him homage. They swore their loyalty in blood drained from their own throats, yielding him eternal power to rule over them as king. They recognized that "his command shall be pre-eminent above and below". Eventually Marduk agreed to punish only their ringleader. So the god Kingu, who had incited the goddess Tiamat to revolt, was bound, and the total crime was laid upon him. The punishment included the letting of his blood—he had to cut his own throat. Marduk then created man from Kingu's blood. Thus it was that man, as the offspring of Kingu (made from clay mixed with his blood), could only be evil. He was to be subject to every whim of the gods, a servile creature quite unlike the noble being whom God created, as we read in Genesis.

The whole epic is very different from the magnificent story of creation as it is recorded in Genesis. The Babylonian account contains much crude mythology, and it certainly cannot be accepted by intelligent people given a choice between the Bible account and this story from Babylonia. The more we study the Bible record the more we are impressed that *here* we have the original, and that, at best, the Babylonian story is a distortion and a corruption of that original.

THE IMPACT OF THE
EBLA TABLETS

That being the case, what is the impact of the new Ebla version of creation? The impact is great indeed. No longer can it be argued (on fallacious grounds anyway) that the Bible story is merely an improved copy of the Babylonian version. Here at Ebla is a version already "purified", but already in written form many hundreds of years before the Babylonian version.

Clearly it is the Babylonian story that has become distorted and corrupted. The Bible record of creation is seen for what it is. The original record is a writing in very ancient times, uncorrupted and majestically acceptable to those who will believe in the great Creator God.

Summarizing, the impact of this tablet from Ebla, with its several copies, is very great. The comment above, "A first-millennium oral Hebrew tradition, in a third-millennium written document," is a telling indication of the impact of such a written record. Here we are—on the other side of Moses by a thousand years, and that means over 2,000 years the other side of Solomon, and a tablet remarkably similar to the commencement of Genesis Chapter 1 is found. Clearly, that "Hebrew tradition" is not oral after all, but has been in writing through the centuries. No longer can it be claimed that this "tradition" dates to only a few hundred years before Christ in its written form. Whether there was an ethnic connection with the Hebrews or not, the tablet from Eber makes it clear that the Bible's creation record is not a camp-fire story, nor was it re-told, embellished, or even purified over the centuries. It is an actual written document, its original predating Abraham by some centuries.

Chapter 5
Ebla
and the Flood

We have seen that Professor Pettinato discussed technical aspects and linguistic problems in relation to a number of tablets. In these new records, the Akkadian language, Amorite, and Eblaic come together. Akkad was to the south-east of Ebla, and the Amorites were over to the West, and so Ebla was more or less between the two. The Professor discussed the relationship between these various forms of language and suggested that they might be three branches. But yet, he tells us, they are "surely distinguished languages". I elaborate this in our next chapter in dealing with the Tower of Babel incident.

That relationship between the three languages leads to an interesting thought, but first it is necessary to consider another aspect of background.

AN EMBARRASSING FACT

In his public question and answer period, Professor Freedman also discussed the possible chronological correlation between Eber of Genesis 10 and Eber [Ebrum], King of Ebla. While not endorsing the early Genesis records as totally acceptable "scientifically", Professor Freedman referred to the "embarrassing" fact that the chronology of Genesis fitted remarkably well with the new discoveries. He went on to refer to the closeness of the Ebla creation record to that of the Bible and commented, "This is rather a shock."

To come back to the "thought" above, perhaps to many scholars the findings at Ebla will continue to contain shocks. Let us conjecture for a moment that in fact the early Genesis records contain factual history. That would mean that the Flood took place a relatively short time before the date of the records now recovered. We have seen that we cannot set absolute dates for Ebla, for the two Italian Professors themselves disagreed by about 100 years. Nor can we be dogmatic about absolute dates for the early Genesis records, for it is widely argued that the genealogical lists of Genesis are not complete in the modern

Western sense, but are selections of important persons in the one direct line.

A good illustration of the argument is shown by a comparison of our Lord's genealogy at Matthew Chapter 1 with the earlier part of the same genealogy, at I Chronicles Chapter 3. At least three names are omitted from Matthew's list, for it is a schematic presentation, with names deliberately chosen according to a perfectly legitimate literary pattern.

Nevertheless, although we cannot insist on an absolute date for such events as the Flood and the happenings at Babel, at least we can come to approximations.

After the Flood, Noah's descendants would have been at least as likely to settle in the area we now call Syria (hence Ebla) as they would in the plains way down to the south, in the area the Bible later calls Chaldea. Similarly Syria would be as likely as the Amorite territory across to the West. After the Ark landed at Ararat, it is entirely logical that a major settlement would develop in the areas centering around Ebla to the south, much closer than either of the two other major centers of civilization.

The new tablets strangely bring together the languages of the Sumerians, the Semites (the territory of the Amorites), and the Eblahites. According to Professor Pettinato, they are "surely distinguished languages". They are separate, and yet they have close affinities. Take the language of the Eblahites—it is "pre-Akkadian" but it is also "close to the original Semitic language". Amoritic was in effect a daughter of that "original Semitic".

This is strange. We see that the scribes at Ebla apparently wrote in what was basically one language (pre-Akkadian Sumerian), but read in another language (Semitic Amorite). The languages are all connected, yet they are separate. Is it possible that there is an as yet unexplained link with the three sons of Noah and the spread of civilization in three different directions?

We have already suggested another possibility—is this strange combination and yet distinctiveness of the three languages somehow linked back to that other Biblical incident, the happenings at the time of the Tower of Babel? We do not know. Perhaps further knowledge will be gained as new finds are made at Ebla, as the languages are better understood, and as a body of scholars gain access to this treasure trove from the past.

Certainly the sounds from Ebla will be echoing through the corridors of learning for many years to come.

SIMILARITY TO THE BABYLONIAN FLOOD STORY

The records of Creation and the Flood at

Ebla are on two different tablets. In a question and answer session with scholars, Pettinato said that the flood tablet was quite small, having five columns in all, and it was well preserved. Only two of the columns have yet been translated, and there are difficulties in further translation. One problem is that some of the signs can be translated in more than one way.

Unlike the Creation record, the Flood tablet appears to have close similarity to the Babylonian record contained in one of the tablets of the *Epic of Gilgamesh*. It is relevant to consider that Epic; Gilgamesh himself was the legendary ruler of the ancient city-state of Uruk, and he was supposed to be two-thirds god and one-third man. The Epic of Gilgamesh in its present form did not include the creation narrative. The two records of creation and the flood are included on a more recently recovered series of tablets known as the Epic of Atrahasis.

Briefly the story of the flood in this Epic of Gilgamesh is as follows: Utnapishtim was the Babylonian Noah, and with his boat-man Puzu-Amurri, he went through seven days of terrible flood. A very good friend of Gilgamesh named Enkidu had died at the decree of the gods, and Gilgamesh realized that he too must eventually die. He heard of Utnapishtim who had escaped death and he set out to find him so that he could learn from him the secret of immortality. Gilgamesh eventually found Utnapishtim, the only man who had ever obtained everlasting life. Gilgamesh asked Utnapishtim how he found this secret of life everlasting. Utnapishtim then told how one of the gods urged him to destroy his house and build a vessel. Utnapishtim obeyed the voice of the gods and built a great boat, and eventually the expected flood came.

GODS COWERING LIKE DOGS AND A WEEPING GODDESS

In the Epic of Gilgamesh we read this: "Even the gods were afeared at the deluge, took to flight and went up to the heaven of Anu, cowered they like dogs and crouched down at the outer defences." That is a very different concept of God from that given in the Bible record of the flood. We could not think of the God of the Bible cowering like dogs or being terrified by a deluge.

Another translation of the epic tells of the goddess Ishtar in great distress: "Ishtar cried like a woman in travail, wailed the queen of the gods with her beautiful voice: 'Those creatures are turned to clay, since I commanded evil in the assembly of the gods; because I commanded evil in the assembly of the gods, for the destruction of my people I commanded battle. I alone bore my people; like spawn of fishes they fill the sea.' The gods along with the Anunnaki wept with her, the gods bowed, sat as they wept; closed were their lips (silent their) assembly." (See "Buried History," *Quarterly Journal of The Australian Institute of Archaeology,* March 1968, p. 26.)

The crude polytheism of this Babylonian epic is obviously vastly different from the majestic, yet simple, Bible record.

When the flood was all over and Utnapishtim came out, he made an offering to the gods, and the Epic of Gilgamesh tells us, "And the gods smelled the savor, the gods smelled the sweet savor, the gods gathered like flies about the priest of the offering." These poor gods had not been fed—because mankind had been destroyed—and so they gathered like flies as soon as Utnapishtim remembered their need and did something about it! How different all this is from the God who is revealed in Scripture. He does not need the offerings of a man to sate His hunger, nor could we ever imagine it being said of the true God of the heavens that He has come like flies to an offering!

After that the gods were angry among themselves and began to blame each other for their foolishness in bringing this flood on man. It is all so different from the Bible picture of God waiting patiently while a gospel of mercy was preached. The true God acted in judgment only when man continued to reject His ways.

SIMILARITIES TO THE
BABYLONIAN STORY

There are some similarities between this Babylonian story of the flood and that in the Bible. Thus in each record there is supposedly a final revelation to the hero of the flood, warning him that a deluge is coming which is unknown to everyone else. However, in the Bible story, Noah is told to warn others so that they too can accept the way of salvation if they so desire.

In each case the hero builds a vessel which is pitched within and without with pitch, describes the flood in which all others are destroyed, tells of the great ship resting on a mountain, and of certain birds being sent out. Each record tells how the hero disembarks and offers a sacrifice, and it then says that such a deluge shall not be visited on man again.

However, the Bible account is very different from the Babylonian legend. The gross polytheism of the Babylonian story, with gods crouching with fear, and then swarming like hungry flies to a sacrifice, is quite alien to the noble concept of the almighty God presented in the Bible record.

OTHER FLOOD STORIES

There is one fragment of the Babylonian flood story which was found at Nippur, and it dates to before 2000 B.C. We saw that another similar legend (the Epic of Atrahasis) has recently been translated, and when we compare these versions with the Bible record, it becomes clear that the Bible is infinitely superior. It does not bear the marks of the grotesque, the superstitious, or the magical. Its description is picturesque, but acceptable to the man or the woman prepared to accede to the great concept of a God who can and does reveal Himself.

Part of the Epic of Gilgamesh was found in the excavations at Megiddo in ancient Palestine (now Israel). It was about a thousand years earlier than that known in the palace of the Assyrian king, Ashurbanipal. This showed that the story was widely known through the Fertile Crescent in patriarchal times. How did that story get from Babylon to Palestine? Clearly someone who traveled the long route had taken this clay tablet with him. And, if that could be done with other ancient stories known in Mesopotamia, why not with the Bible stories? Abraham migrated across that same Fertile Crescent not so very long before the date of this particular copy of the Babylonian flood story, and he too could well have carried original tablets which Moses eventually used to give us the early stories in Genesis. Certainly the Bible records were *not* copied from those in the palace of the Assyrian king, Ashurbanipal—as formerly claimed. As Professor W. F. Albright points out (*In Yahweh and the Gods of Canaan,* p. 86), the Bible record contains archaic features dating it to before any Mesopotamian version that is "preserved in cuneiform sources."

A COPY OF THE BABYLONIAN STORY IN ISRAEL

A fragment of the Babylonian *Epic of Gilgamesh* was found when the northern Israel city of Megiddo was being excavated, and this dated to about 1400 B.C. The interesting point was then raised, that if this Babylonian epic could be carried across the Fertile Crescent at a date close to Patriarchal times, why could not the same be true of the early Bible narratives?

That becomes an even more likely proposition when we further consider the relationship of King Eber to the Genesis tablets and the possible relationship of this Ebrum King of Ebla to the Hebrew people of a later time. This we do in our chapter headed. "Who was Ebrum, King of Ebla"?

The evidence could be multiplied as to the superiority of the Bible records of creation and the flood. However, more than superiority has been demonstrated. It has also become clear that the records were in writing much earlier than seemed possible a generation ago when so many scholars believed that the Bible versions were put in writing long after the time of Solomon.

Chapter 6
Was Ebla Contemporary With Babel?

This vast empire of Ebla was contemporary with the first dynasty of Akkad and was a competitor with that power until Naram-Sin finally conquered Ebla about 2250 B.C.

This possibly brings us back to the very time of the Tower of Babel: Professor Albright was one scholar who believed that incident should be dated to the time of Sargon of Akkad, the grandfather of Naram-Sin who eventually took control of Ebla. Professor Freedman refers to this possible association in his report on the new findings.

It is relevant to state that there have been other scholarly probings on this matter of the Tower of Babel, and it is being increasingly recognized that this

The village currently known as Ebla near the Tell Mardikh.

Photo courtesy of Robert Durnal.

strange happening cannot be glibly written off after all.

I elaborate the new approach to this incident in *That Incredible Book the Bible*. It is included here as background to the story of Ebla.

At Genesis Chapter 11 we hear people saying to each other, "Go to, let us build a city and a tower, whose top may reach unto heaven; and let us make us a name, lest we be scattered abroad upon the face of the whole earth."

Ancient peoples often build their cities around their sacred towers. That was what Sir Leonard Woolley found when he excavated at the city of Ur, and it has been found in many other places too. With the successful development of furnaced bricks, much bigger buildings were possible than before with stones, and so men now decided to build this great tower toward heaven.

Possibly they were thinking of being safe in case another flood judgment came; certainly they were setting themselves up as a super people, and their tower would not be to the glory of God. This becomes clear by the excavations of later towers. The actual pattern of ancient temple towers was to have the shrine of the god at the top, and thus it was the focal point, the center of attention. Little wonder that God was displeased, for such a temple spoke of rejection of the true God. And in this first temple at Babel we find the seeds of rebellion and self-glorification, fully developed in later times. When we look at the great ziggurat, or temple tower, at the city of Ur—which was in this same general area—we find that it contained an inner shrine where all sorts of abominable practices were carried out in the name of the moon-god Nannar.

No longer do scholars disregard this story, for modern research has clearly demonstrated that many civilizations did indeed have their beginnings from Mesopotamia. Archaeology confirms that the influence and the culture of Mesopotamia spread far and wide as men scattered abroad upon the face of the earth. In this general pattern of the spread of culture, archaeology supports the story. It is well attested also that many of the languages known in the Ancient Near East were actually developed in the general area of Mesopotamia, the plain of Shinar.

Professor W. F. Albright suggested that the story should be dated to the twenty-second century B.C. and that the word "sem" does not mean "name" but "an [inscribed] monument". He says, "It was, therefore, as a tremendous monument to its builders that the Tower of Babel was intended," (*Yahweh and the gods of Canaan,* p. 87).

It was a sad picture. Man's rebellion and self-glorification led once again to the judgment of God, not by a flood this time, but his language was confused and he was scattered throughout the earth.

THE SITE OF BABEL

The question is often asked, "Is the site of the Tower of Babel known today?" The answer is, opinions differ.

There is a large water-hole at the site of Nebuchadnezzar's famous city of Babylon. Some scholars claim that this was the site of the Tower of Babel and that its bricks have been used for nearby building activities. However, it might have been a later tower.

Others suggest that ancient Kish, a few miles from Babylon, is the correct site. Others again suggest a third nearby site, Birs-Nimrud, the ancient Borsippa. But no one really knows. The pattern of "ziggurats", or temple-towers, is, however, well attested in these areas of the East.

It is interesting that other peoples also have traditions as to the Tower of Babel. Robert T. Boyd writes:

> "Not only has the discovery of many ziggurats helped to confirm the Biblical record of a tower at Babel, but further evidence relates a story of King Ur-Nammu of the Third Dynasty of Ur (2044 to 2007 B.C.). He received orders from his god and goddess to build the ziggurat. The stele is nearly five feet across

and ten feet high. At the top, the king stands in an attitude of prayer. Above his head is the symbol of the moon god Nannar and to the right are figures of angels with vases from which flow the streams of life (the earliest known artistic figures of angels). The panels show the king setting out with compass, pick and trowel, and mortar baskets to begin construction. One panel preserves only a ladder used as the structure was rising. The reverse side records a commemorative feast.

"A clay tablet was unearthed which gave the following account of a ziggurat: 'The erection [building] of this tower [temple] highly offended all the gods. In a night they [threw down] what man had built and impeded their progress. They were scattered abroad, and their speech was strange.' Once again the archaeologist has given to us evidence that the Bible records and accounts of other peoples of other nations are closely related, and that the Bible is not just a 'one-sided' account of events and happenings." (In *Tells, Tombs and Treasures.*)

THE CONFUSION OF TONGUES

One final point. The March, 1968, *Journal of the American Oriental Society* consists of a series of essays in memory of the famous archaeologist E. A. Speiser, and one essay is by Professor S. N. Kramer, of the University of Pennsylvania: *"The 'Babel of Tongues'*—A Sumerian Version." Dr. Kramer reminds us that E. A. Speiser analyzed with characteristic acumen, learning, and skill the Mesopotamian background of the "Tower of Babel" narrative and came to the conclusion that it "had a demonstrable source in cuneiform literature" (pp. 74-76 *Anchor Bible* "Genesis").

Professor Speiser was by no means alone in this view, e.g. Professor Robert Braidwood was another. He referred to the widespread acceptance of a factual basis to much about early civilization that had previously been regarded as purely mythical.

Dr. Kramer says of his own article: "This paper will help to corroborate and confirm Speiser's conclusion by bringing to light a new parallel to one of the essential motifs in the 'Tower of Babel' theme—the confusion of tongues."

Another essay in the same series tells of a fragmentary tablet of 27 lines that has recently been copied by the Oxford cuneiformist Oliver Gurney. This helps to restore the idea of a golden age, an idea known in literature for about 25 years. This "golden age" was supposed to have been in the earlier Sumerian period. The new fragmentary tablet includes a Sumerian version of the story of the Babel of tongues. This "golden age" passage is actually part of an address where an unknown ruler wants "the lord of Arrata" to allow him to become his vassal and then to have gold, silver, and semiprecious stones procured in order to build various shrines and temples, with a special emphasis on the great temple in the city of Eridu.

Here is the translation as it relates to this Sumerian version of the time when there was only one language:

> "Once upon a time there was no
>   snake, there was no scorpion,
> There was no hyena, there was no
>   lion,
> There was no wild dog, no wolf.
> There was no fear, no terror.
> Man had no rival.
> In those days, the lands Subur
>   and Hamazi,
> Harmony-tongued Sumer, the
>   great land of the decrees of
>   princeship,
> Uri, the land having all that is appropriate.
> The land Martu, resting in security,
> The whole universe, the people in
>   unison
> To Enlil in one tongue. . . ."

Clearly, men believed in a golden age when they were free from fear and want, living in a world that knew nothing but prosperity. All the people of the world worshipped one god, it being claimed in this story that he was the Sumerian god Enlil. They were able to speak to their god in one tongue, as we are told in the last line above.

This is not the first tablet in which there is a reference to speaking in one tongue, but this new tablet is actually a better preserved copy of the previously known Epic tale "Emmerkar and the Lord of Aratta," published by Dr. Kramer in 1952 as a monograph of the University of Pennsylvania Museum. However, until this tablet was translated the meaning was ambigious—it could have been taken literally to suggest that all the peoples of the world did indeed use the same language, or it could have been looked at as a figurative expression declaring the unanimity of all people as they acknowledged the supremacy of Enlil.

This text makes it clear that people were indeed supposed to speak but one language.

As Dr. Kramer says:

> "Our new piece, therefore, puts it beyond all doubt that the Sumerians believed that there was a time when all mankind spoke one and the same language, and that it was Enki, the Sumerian god of wisdom, who

confounded their speech. The reason for this fateful deed is not stated in the text; it may well have been inspired by Enki's jealousy of Enlil and the universal sway over mankind that he enjoyed."

In the quote above, Professor Albright suggested the 22nd century B.C. as the time of this incident, whereas the Ebla findings point to a somewhat earlier date for Sargon. The evidence is not conclusive. It is not finally established that the Tower of Babel IS to be dated to the time of Sargon: my point is that the incident is discussed in academic circles today as something more than mythology.

Often Bible stories have seemed to be incredible, but later evidence has vindicated the record. It is seen as sober history after all.

SOME QUESTIONS ABOUT BABEL AND EBLA

It is relevant to ask another question: Are the strange relationships, yet differences, between the languages of the Sumerians, the Semites, and the Eblahites somehow associated with the Tower of Babel incident? They were three distinct languages, yet they had a definite interrelationship. At Genesis 11:9 we read this:

> "Therefore is the name of it
> called Babel; because the Lord
> did there confound the language
> of all the earth: and from thence
> did the Lord scatter them abroad
> upon the face of all the earth."

These people were one until the Babel incident, according to Genesis Chapter 11.
Then two things happened:

1. Their language was confounded
2. They were scattered to many places

Does this explain why there were three
languages associated with Ebla and the
other two major contemporary
civilizations? Is it the reason why some
"Hebrews" (the Terah/Abraham branch)
were in the area of the two rivers, while
others of the clan were found to the north,
possibly in association with Ebla?

Is it why the earliest level so far
recovered at Ebla coincides with the first
(not the second) dynasty at Akkad? Did
these civilizations commence contem-
poraneously at a time when there was a
sudden dispersal of many peoples, just as
Genesis 11:9 says? If we accept Genesis
11:9 as factual, this new commencement
actually happened at some time in history.
I do not know, but it is at least possible that
the findings at Ebla are linked with that
early historical period. The new tablets at
Ebla lead to questions such as these.

When further scholarly work has been
done and more of the tablets are

translated, it is likely that we will again be surprised at the clues within scripture. Light from archaeology serves to bring out those hidden clues, silently resting in the Sacred Record until in God's time the searchlight of truth enhances their brilliance.

For it is still true that "truth shall spring from the earth" (Psalm 85:11).

Chapter 7
Who Was Ebrum, King of Ebla?

In the *Biblical Archaeologist* mentioned earlier, Professor Pettinato lists the names of the kings of Ebla, as follows:

Igrish-Halam
Ar-Ennum
Ebrum
Ibbi-Sippish
Dubuhu-Ada
Irkab-Damu

Although the details are not very clear, it is established that Ebrum and his two successors are respectively father, son, and grandson.

The Professor goes on to suggest that Ebrum is possibly the same name as Eber. The "resemblance to Eber, the father of the Semites according to Genesis 10:21, is truly surprising." He suggests an alternative reading of Eb-ri-um, "which inevitably elicits *'ibri,* Hebrew'." The Professor suggests that the second use of the word is more likely.

This possible identification with Eber or with the Hebrews is one of the major reasons why the tablets from Ebla have already become famous and are of special interest to Bible students.

In *Time* magazine of October 18, 1976, Professor Freedman is quoted as stating:

> "We always thought of ancestors like Eber as symbolic. Nobody ever regarded them as historic—at least, not until this tablet was found. Fundamentalists could have a field day with this one."

"THE TABLE OF NATIONS" IN GENESIS

Actually it is not accurate to say that "nobody ever regarded them as historic." In *Recent Discoveries in Bible Lands* (pp. 70ff.), Professor Albright wrote about the "Table of Nations" at Genesis Chapter 10 as "an astonishingly accurate document". Eber is named there, at verse 25. He takes his place in this "astonishingly accurate document."

Because of the possible association of Ebrum with the Table of Nations, we quote

Professor Albright's comment at this point:

> "It stands absolutely alone in ancient literature without a remote parallel even among the Greeks. . . . 'The Table of Nations' remains an astonishingly accurate document. . . . [It] shows such remarkably 'modern' understanding of the ethnic and linguistic situation in the modern world, in spite of all its complexity, that scholars never fail to be impressed with the author's knowledge of the subject."

Archaeology has given clear testimony to the accuracy of the chapter, for nearly all the names mentioned are now known. The Bible records have been substantiated in no uncertain manner, not only as regards the people who are in the center of Biblical history, but as regards many other peoples as well. The Assyrians, the Medes, the Greeks, the Egyptians, and many others are mentioned, and in many ways that are very precise and accurate. We even find reference to points that were long ago forgotten, but are now known to have been just as the Bible briefly states. One example is that Nineveh was established by the rulers of Babylon, stated in Genesis 10:1 and 12. This is in harmony with what the monuments tell us.

Other nations, such as the Greeks, had

stories as to the origins of peoples, but they are clearly mythological. The Bible "Table of Nations" is unique and is another strong pointer to the fact that Bible records stand alone among the documents of ancient times.

Only the Bible gives an acceptable history of a people from its actual development through individuals. Most other peoples start their written histories only when they are well established, with powerful kings ruling, and the nation's early beginnings lost in antiquity. By comparison the Hebrew people have a remarkable outline as to their origins in the early chapters of Genesis.

THE EBLA KING LIST
DIFFERS FROM GENESIS

I seriously challenge the possibility of King Ebrum of Ebla being the Eber of Genesis Chapter 10. The names of the kings before and after Ebrum are not the same as those in Genesis Chapter 10, and this immediately raises problems. It does not entirely rule out the possibility of the two being equated, for it was common-place for rulers to have alternative names. However, the Genesis 10 list is clearly of men who are in the same direct lineage, whereas the Ebla list is of the kings of that city, but they are not all in the same family line.

Another highly relevant point is that

Eber, his predecessors and his successors all lived for great periods of time.

We learn from archaeology that there are traditions about men living for great lengths of time, and there is strong evidence as to the historical basis of these traditions. The so-called "Sumerian King List" tells of long-living kings who lived "before the flood". According to the ancient historian Berossus, those kings reigned for periods ranging from 10,800 years to 64,800 years each, and the grand total is 432,000. In view of these great periods of time, the Bible figures are not so strange after all. Of course we cannot accept those Babylonian figures, but when we put them alongside the Bible statements, we are impressed with the conservative nature of the Bible record.

This tradition that men lived for long periods of time is known to many peoples. The Egyptians and the Chinese speak of kings who lived for thousands of years. In the Chinese version there were two semidivine emperors who reigned in early times. The later Greeks and Romans were more conservative in their figures, for they suggested ages from 800 to 1,000 years, reminding us of the Bible figures. The Jewish historian Josephus, who lived at the time of Christ, had no doubts about the authenticity of these long-living early men, and he wrote accepting the traditions of various peoples who united their testimony to this fact.

Climatic changes, the effects of sin and disease, even the social problems of developing civilization, would all play their part in reducing the age limit of man. Diet, too, has probably had its influence. The Bible also indicates that man was nearer to perfection at that time, another important reason why man could live longer.

The fact that we today do not live for 800 or 900 years does not mean that such longevity was never possible. It is sometimes said that Genesis Chapter 1-11, the so-called seed plot of the Bible, is suprahistorical in that it is historical, but set against conditions which are unknown today. We do not know what tremendous climatic or other changes occurred when the Biblical flood took place. We do not know what cataclysmic effects it would have had on past civilizations and cultures—perhaps virtually wiping out all traces of such culture. It could possibly have caused the great climatic changes of which we have clues when we find there was tropical growth at the South Pole, and that the Siberian wastelands of today once were able to provide food for the huge mammals that have been found in recent times with great quantities of grass and vegetation still undigested. There are reputable scholars who seriously suggest that they were suddenly overtaken, possibly by the flood described in detail in the Bible at Genesis Chapters 7 through 9.

It is interesting to notice that the Sumerian King List (with long ages which we acknowledge to be greatly exaggerated) suddenly reduces the reigns of the kings after the flood down to 100 years, and we find a somewhat similar decrease in longevity in the Bible records relating to pre- and post-flood conditions.

KING EBRUM WAS NOT "LONG-LIVING"

In private conversation I asked Professor Pettinato, "Is there any indication in the tablets you have so far deciphered that there were long-living men? — for in the Table of Nations they are shown to have lived for much longer periods than we do today."

Professor Pettinato smiled and then said, "No, they just lived ordinary lives, just like we do today."

The facts bear out this conclusion. There are contemporary cross referencings, such as King Ebrum of Ebla ruling at the same time as Pharaoh Pepi of Egypt. The time of Ebla's end was contemporary with Naram-Sin, and there were three rulers between Ebrum and this final destruction. Put another way, this is also the time between Sargon of Akkad and his grandson Naram-Sin. Clearly this is nothing like the time lapse demanded by the periods referred to in the Bible record.

Thus Ebrum of Ebla is not Eber of Genesis 10.

However, even though the list of kings at Ebla is not the same as the Genesis 10 list, that does not rule out the possibility of there being a direct link between Ebrum and the Hebrew people. The tablets make it clear that from the time of Ebrum there was a new identification with Ya, and this is probably Yahweh. It is entirely feasible that Ebrum was "a Hebrew" who introduced a knowledge of Yahweh to these people and was of such stature that his son and his son's son after him were the rulers of this extensive kingdom.

Sargon of Akkad (the Great) brought Mari into subjection to Akkad and achieved Ebla's subjection also. Professor Pettinato conjectures that this "caused the dismissal of the king Ar-Ennum and favored Ebrum's ascent to the throne." He further points out that even though Ebrum was thought to be weaker than his predecessor, he actually caused greater problems for the empire of Akkad. After Sargon had withdrawn, "Ebrum re-annexed Mari and made one of his own sons king." Sargon's immediate successors were helpless against this tide of events, and "Only under Naram-Sin did Akkad recover well enough to defeat the Eblahites and finally to destroy Ebla itself."

"A WANDERING ARAMEAN"

It is relevant to point out that the Bible speaks of Abraham as "a wandering Aramean". "Aram" was an old name for Syria, and this statement indicates that somehow Abraham was associated with Syria. That is where Ebla was located, and Professor Pettinato's statement that he preferred the word "Hebrew" instead of the personal name "Eber" [Ebrum] would be in keeping with such an interpretation. He further makes the point that "it is not mere chance that precisely under Eber [Ebrum] the state of Ebla reached its greatest splendor, and it was just during his reign that Akkad—so one of the tablets reports—paid tribute to Ebla."

However, as we say previously, Ebrum's family does not appear to have been the royal line of Ebla after the time of Ebrum's grandson. Another king, Irkab-Damu, was on the throne when Naram-Sin finally destroyed the city about 2,250 B.C. At first it might seem that one possibility is that some of the descendants of the royal family of Ebrum journeyed to the south-east at this time, down to another city of the moon god, even to Ur of the Chaldees. On this supposition, some of the forebears of that "wandering Aramean" might have wandered to the land of the two rivers at this time.

Interesting as such a conjecture might

be, it is put forward only because someone is sure to suggest it. The Genesis record seems to rule it out, for in Genesis Chapter 11 we read of men finding a plain and settling in the area of Sumer (Shinar), and Abraham is introduced in that context. One purpose of those first eleven chapters of Genesis is to introduce us to Abraham, and if Ebla was in his background it is probable that the reference to the Plain of Shinar would have been irrelevant.

It is more likely that other "Hebrews" had already migrated north to Ebla, to Haran (see Genesis 27:43), and to the general area of Padan-Aram (Genesis 28:5). Rebecca's father is actually called "Bethuel the Syrian" (Genesis 28:5). As we study the relationships between the Patriarchs, it is clear that they had family ties with people living in that Syrian region, to the north.

This had apparently been the case independently of Abraham's own movements.

Summarizing, it is my conclusion that King Ebrum was not Eber of Genesis 10, but did have some ethnic connection with "Hebrews". These people were known in the land between the two rivers, and also in the areas around Ebla. They apparently had some knowledge of the great God Ya, Whom later Hebrews knew by his fuller name of Yahweh.

Chapter 8
The Delusion of
the Documentary
Hypothesis

To analyze one of the most important aspects of the Ebla tablets, we must first understand at least the basis of the so-called Documentary Hypothesis. In my next chapter we shall see how the Ebla tablets are relevant to this hypothesis.

Contrary to the belief sometimes expressed by non-scholars, academics are not always guilty of deliberately burying their heads in the sand. My personal experience with archaeologists has been that they fight tenaciously for their particular standpoint, but once evidence is conclusive they put their theory to one side and move on to other fields of conquest.

That is strangely not the case with many scholars in their approach to the documents of the Bible. The problem is that ultimately there are only two opposite positions that can be held, though of course there are variations as to the specifics of the two points of view. They are that the Bible is inspired of God in a special sense, or it is simply the biased history of the Jewish (and then Christian) people.

At this point we do not elaborate many of the variations between the two "camps". Our purpose is to see the relevance of the Ebla tablets to the Bible documents, and, to do that, it is necessary to have at least a basic outline of the Documentary Hypothesis. I stress that what follows was the basic hypothesis, and there have been many variations and modifications in recent years, as one aspect after another ultimately has been shown to be unacceptable.

This hypothesis began to come into prominence in the 1840's, and in that same decade the first of the great Assyrian palaces were unearthed. The documents recovered from libraries such as that of the Assyrian King Ashurbanipal showed in various ways that the Bible writings were historical documents. Assyrian copies of Babylonian Epics of Creation and the Flood were studied, and eventually it was realized that the Bible records were superior, and that they were also considerably older.

One major claim of this Hypothesis was that the Patriarchal Narratives were originally camp-fire stories that grew in the telling, and that the records about Abraham and Isaac were two different strands of separate legends, with the two chief characters simply idealized figures, conveniently brought together as father and son.

Such an argument is nonsense. Recovered documents have made it clear that the Patriarchal Narratives must be taken seriously, as eye-witness source documents. They combine with other evidence to show that the case of the Documentary Hypothesis against the Bible has dismally failed.

WHAT THE DOCUMENTARY HYPOTHESIS IS ALL ABOUT

The Documentary Hypothesis theorizes that various tribal laws and stories were known amongst the early Israelite people and were passed down by word of mouth through the centuries, until at last they were committed to writing in the centuries following Solomon, eventually being brought together as part of their national literature. The Ten Commandments, the Book of the Covenant as found in Exodus 21-23, the Song of Moses in Deuteronomy 32, and the ancient Song of Deborah in Judges 5 (often regarded by higher critics as the earliest literary composition in the Old Testament) are all supposed to have been among the early pieces of Israelite writing which eventually became incorporated in the volumes of national literature.

The Documentary Hypothesis is put forward to explain the origins of all Old Testament writings, but one of its primary interests has been in its contentions relating to the origins of the Torah ("Teaching") or "Pentateuch"—the first five books of the Bible. It claims that these books are actually writings brought together from many sources, which were first known as a compilation of written documents many hundreds of years after the death of Moses.

The first two streams of writing were supposed to be the documents "J" (for Jehovah) and "E" (for Elohim) which had been used in the compilation of Genesis. The theory was soon extended, and it was hypothesized that "J" and "E" were spread throughout ALL the Old Testament, with other documents incorporated from time to time.

THE THEORY AS TO "J" AND "E"

According to the theory, a collection of tribal stories and other "legends", etc., eventually emerged from among the southern tribes, and this was the document "J", dated somewhere around 900 to 850 B.C.—that is to say, not long after the death of Solomon.

The Documentary Hypothesis further argued that a second document, "E", emerged from the tribes in the North somewhere about 750 B.C. Thus this collection is supposed to have been brought together as such only about a generation before Israel was taken into captivity in 721 B.C. The theory clearly does not allow sufficient time for these records to have been accepted as an authoritative part of the nation's sacred writings, especially when there was such feeling between Israel to the north and Judah to the south.

The theory goes on to suggest that an editor or a Redactor (R) combined these into a single collection, referred to as "J/E", somewhere about 650 B.C. How the northern and the southern writers combined with such singleness of purpose, in view of the historical situation, is not explained.

By now the work of the prophets had become important, and according to the Documentary Hypothesis the essential religious beliefs of Israel actually originated with the prophets. The theory suggests that earlier doctrines were known to the Covenant People, but that "more advanced" teachings such as monotheism were only arrived at over long centuries of religious development. This is where the work of the prophets is supposed to have fitted in, as each prophet and his followers added their contribution.

According to this theory, the influence of the prophets of the 8th and 7th centuries B.C. was such that many new religious ideas were now developed. Thus it was these prophets who first realized there was a covenant relationship with God, so that prosperity and righteousness were linked, as also were misfortunes and sinfulness. This is supposed to have led them to a new understanding of the importance of ethics, and what we now know as "Ethical Monotheism" became recognized—that God was a holy God, the One true God Who expected His people to accept and practice His Own standards of holiness. Isaiah is the prophet who is credited with bringing this into most general acceptance.

THE DOCUMENT "D"

This new approach to doctrine and this "philosophy of religion" were brought in with the Document "D" which the prophets are said to have composed, or to have been responsible for, somewhere about 650 B.C. It is argued that this was the document which Hilkiah found in the Temple in 621 B.C., leading to immediate reforms.

The work of Professor George Mendenhall of Michigan is highly relevant at this point. One of the six points with Covenants dating to the second millennium B.C. was the depositing of a copy in the sanctuary. That is exactly what happened with this copy of part of the Law of Moses.

It was found where it was supposed to be found.

This work "D" is regarded basically as the Book of Deuteronomy—especially chapters 12 to 26—and its proclamation in the time of Josiah was supposed to be the very first reading of a Book that was then to be authoritatively declared as canonical. The earlier traditional view, of course, is that this was simply a genuine rediscovery and a consequent re-establishment of the sadly-neglected but ancient "Law of Moses". This is the straightforward statement as it is found at II Kings 22 and 23. According to the Documentary Hypothesis the story in those chapters is simply a "pious fraud".

There are many evidences that Deuteronomy was written long before the time of Josiah. The people are clearly being instructed against a time and background which is very different from the extensive development of Josiah's time; and some of the laws, e.g. concerning two wives at Deuteronomy 21:15ff., would have been looked on quite differently by the time of Josiah. This particular law reflects actual customs of Moses' time, for even the great leader Moses had to recognize "the hardness of heart" of the people (see Matthew 19:8ff.). Interestingly enough, this provision in Deuteronomy has a near-parallel in the Code of Hammurabi and this becomes a relative dating point, suggesting the genuine antiquity of this writing. By Josiah's time such a position would have been faced in a different way by the various prophets.

A possible brief historical reconstruction is as follows:

First, in Deuteronomy itself there is the claim that Moses (and not the later prophets) wrote it. Moses gave instructions to the priests for it to be placed beside (or in the side of) the Ark of the Covenant and to be read regularly to the assembled people, as shown at Deuteronomy 31:9-13, 24-29.

It is interesting to put these verses alongside II Kings 22:8:

> "And Hilkiah the high priest said unto Shaphan the scribe, I have found the book of the law in the house of the Lord. And Hilkiah gave the book to Shaphan, and he read it."

There is no real reason to doubt the veracity of the Bible record, and so-called "pious frauds" in Scripture have a habit of proving to be remarkably accurate writing of history. Ezra the Scribe and Luke the beloved physician are perhaps the best two examples of Bible writers being seriously discredited, so it seemed, and then being re-established so that "liberal" and "conservative" alike came to recognize each of them as first-class historians, even by secular standards.

According to the Documentary Hypothesis as regards Document "D", considerable editorial work was carried out by redactors who combined "J", "E", and "D". To these documents they constantly introduced additional prophetic material up to about 550 B.C.

THE HOLINESS CODE "H" AND THE PRIESTLY LEGISLATION "P"

Next came the priestly group, and they were supposed to have produced the Law of Holiness, the code known as "H", basically Leviticus 17-20.

Later, after the exile, this priestly school is supposed to have produced a longer account of Israel's history, including a considerable amount of priestly legislation. This priestly legislation is said to be the document "P", supposedly forming a framework for the final compilation of the Torah, the five books of Moses, into which the documents "J/E", "D", and "H" were also incorporated by the redactor (R), about 400 B.C.

The Documentary Hypothesis sometimes extends the Pentateuch to a Hexateuch (i.e. six books, instead of five as in the Pentateuch). The argument is that Joshua should be included because the sources JED and P are prominent in this book also.

Various other additions and redactions

are supposed to have taken place, with an Edomite source known as "S", a Kenite source known as "K"—and so it goes on, with almost as many divisions and subdivisions as there have been "experts" deciding the sources. They have contradicted each other very considerably, and their theories are notoriously subject to revision.

DIFFERENT NAMES FOR GOD

We said that originally one of the main bases for analyzing and dating these documents was the way different names were used for God, thus if God is called Jehovah, it is a "J" section, if He is referred to as Elohim, it is an "E" portion. However, to make the system consistent it was necessary to break up the Old Testament into all sorts of strange combinations, with single verses broken into sections, and then for parts of those sentences to be credited to different documents, according to whether God was known as "J" or "E".

Ultimately, the whole system of source determination based on the Divine Names was seen to be quite untenable—so much so that even one of its greatest exponents, Professor S.R. Driver, eventually stated that the use of Divine Names as a criterion for analysis was not basic to the argument of the Documentary Hypothesis. (Yet this use of the Divine Names was basic to the whole theory originally.)

The Ras Shamra tablets on the coast of Syria pointed to a similar conclusion as to the use of divine names. From those tablets it became obvious that names of various gods were sometimes used interchangeably. The Israelite practice was in keeping with the literary forms of the time.

SUPPOSEDLY DIFFERENT "STYLES"

The second reason for such an analysis is based on style, it being argued that "J" is a simple unaffected narrative, as in his anthropomorphism (presenting the actions of God in human form—hands, eyes, ears, etc.). The writer of "E" is supposed not to be as perfect in his form as "J", though displaying great skill in presenting human nature. Document "D" is said to be elaborate in style, where "P" is looked on as a systematic and prosaic writer, with special interest in such things as genealogies, chronology, measurements, and priestly rituals.

The Documentary Hypothesis claims far too much, and over and over again it does not understand basic approaches to Scripture. It quotes apparent differences—such as the supposed problems in the order of creation in Genesis 1 when compared with

Genesis 2—as an argument for different authorship. However (to comment on that particular question), the Biblical approach very often is to present the basic facts in an outline form and then proceed to elaborate certain aspects. The story of creation is merely an example of a general picture being presented first, with the details filled in a little later. It is not two differing accounts, but an elaboration of what had already been given in outline. The total picture of all creation is first given, followed by details of the particular subject of special interest — man.

A similar presentation is where the history of Esau's descendants is told in brief outline (at Genesis 36), and then the history comes back, at Chapter 37, to deal in far greater detail with Jacob who has a much more important place in the Biblical record than Esau.

DOUBLETS

We have already referred to the two records of creation, and another argument often put forward for the Documentary Hypothesis is that there are apparent doublets (two different records of the one event). However, when we look at them more closely these doublets are seen to be complementary and supplementary, but not contradictory.

Another example is the account of the flood, which is supposed to be a doublet, told separately by "J" and "P"; it is argued that Genesis 7 contradicts Chapter 6, there being a pair of each animal in Chapter 6, and seven pairs of animals in Genesis 7:2. However, Chapter 7 is a later instruction as Noah and his family are about to embark. The "seven" applies to clean animals only (see Genesis 7:2), of which only ten different varieties (for sacrifice) are mentioned in Exodus. Also, the word "pair" is actually a collective and could not be further pluralized. It could have implied more than two.

Joseph being sold into slavery is another supposed "doublet," recorded by "J" and "E", with the two accounts being brought together as one at Genesis Chapter 37. Contradictions are suggested as to whether Reuben or Judah was active in the disposal of Joseph (cf. verse 22 with verse 26), but verse 29 makes it clear that Reuben was not party to Joseph being sold into Egypt. Joseph was sold to "Ishmeelites" according to verses 25, 27, 28, but it is "Midianites" at verses 28 and 36. Actually both tribes were traders, and they could have been in the one caravan, and in any case the "Midianites" were a branch of the "Ishmeelites." There simply is no contradiction.

VARIATIONS IN HIGHER CRITICAL APPROACH

There are variations and extensions of the Documentary Hypothesis, but none of them is really any more satisfying than the approach we have already looked at. The basic argument is to suggest that there was primitive religion in the early Bible writings—a religion with society as a simple community under elders.

Next there is supposed to be a stage of "prophetism" where the concept of the one true God is recognized. An ethnical note creeps into this agricultural society, and their religion is becoming more institutionalized—climaxed in Josiah's reign.

The third stage is supposed to bring us to the priestly emphasis which came into prominence during the exile with Ezekiel, followed by the later priestly group led by Ezra the Scribe who did so much in the post-exilic years, so the theory claimed, to evolve an exclusive worship of Judah. Thus is was that the priests became the dominant class.

A FINAL LOOK AT THE PENTATEUCH: THE TRADITIONAL VIEW

The original traditional view is that the Pentateuch is basically Mosaic in authorship, and there is no strong reason to depart from the view. There is evidence within the Pentateuch that Moses kept records, at Exodus 17:8-14, 24:4-7, Numbers 33:2, Deuteronomy 31:9-12, and in other places.

The uniform testimony of centuries of tradition endorsed the Mosaic authorship, and an abundance of historical and archaeological evidence now points to the great accuracy of the early writings. This has in fact re-established the authenticity of these books in a way that seemed impossible in the days when Wellhausen was so strongly opposing the Mosaic authorship, back in the 1870's. The findings at sites such as Ur, Nuzi, Mari, Kish, Ras Shamra, and Bogazkhoi do much to confirm the accuracy of the stories in Genesis. Similarly the authentic background to the Joseph and Moses records in Egypt is well-established.

It has become clear that it certainly is still possible to look on Moses as the one who compiled Genesis, probably from written records such as those of Genesis Chapters 14 and 23, and other tablets handed on through the descendants of Abraham. Moses also was the author of extensive records, both law and history, as we see in the Bible's own claims.

A careful study of the records suggests that at times there were editing notes, often to make things applicable to or understood by many generations, instead of only the generation to whom the writing was given in the first place. The person prepared to do some Bible searching will find that Genesis 14:2, 3, 7, 8; Genesis 36:31; Exodus 16:35; Exodus 11:3; Numbers 12:3; Numbers 21:14, and Deuteronomy 34 all illustrate this. Numbers 32:34 ff.; and Deuteronomy 2:12 are also relevant.

This does not detract from or affect the significance of the Bible as revelation from God, for the same Holy Spirit who inspired the writings of Moses could just as surely direct the hands of those who were privileged to add editing notes as they brought these things up to date for later generations.

JEWISH TRADITION ABOUT MOSES

Ancient Jewish tradition, which universally accepts the Mosaic authorship of the Pentateuch, also credits Joshua with some editing. There is actually a note to this effect as regards Deuteronomy, in the Syriac version. This could explain similarities of style between Deuteronomy and Joshua and would probably tell us who added the note at the end of Deuteronomy relating to the death of Moses.

Such a view would not allow for the compilation of the Torah centuries later, for Joshua was, for example, written while Rahab was still alive (Joshua 6:25). Moses wrote the Law in a book and kept a record of history (Exodus 17:14; 24:4; Numbers 33:2. See also Mark 12:26). At times Moses actually dated his "diary", as when he talked about "the fifteenth day of the second month" (Exodus 16:1).

It is quite possible that Moses used other helpers as his amanuenses, as the Apostle Paul did centuries later. Moses might well have used such helpers as his "servant" Joshua, or his high-priestly brother Aaron, but the author is ultimately Moses himself. He was the one who was inspired by the Holy Spirit of God to give us these writings.

Right through the Old Testament we find the Torah referred to as Mosaic, as a glance at a concordance under "Moses" makes clear, e.g. I Kings 2:3.

Christ Himself credited Moses with those writings. He referred, not just to the Law, but to the law of Moses (Luke 24:44) and quoted Moses as author (Matthew 19:8, John 7:19, etc.). When He spoke of "the book of Moses" (Mark 12:26) surely He meant just that and clearly endorsed the universally-held Jewish view that Moses was literally the author of the Torah. This was certainly the Jewish view, even as early as Joshua, as shown for example at Joshua 8:31: "As Moses the servant of the Lord commanded the children of Israel, as it is written in the BOOK [emphasis added] of the law of Moses, . . ." There are many such references —Joshua 1:7, 8; II

Chronicles 25:4; Ezra 6:18; Nehemiah 13:1, to mention a few.

WHY NOT ACCEPT THE BIBLE'S OWN STATEMENTS?

The bases put forward for dating source documents are far too often manipulated to fit the particular theory, rather than taking the facts as they are presented in Scripture, and then seeing if they cannot be accepted at their face value. Very often the real problem is not that there are contradictions within the Old Testament, but it is the complete unpreparedness of scholars to recognize the *possibility*—let alone the *fact*—of divine inspiration and revelation.

In any case, the Documentary Hypothesis and its variants grossly neglect established principles for the understanding of ancient history. The interested reader will find those brilliantly outlined in Kenneth Kitchen's *Ancient Orient And The Old Testament* (Inter Varsity Press, Chicago, 1966).

Chapter 9
Pointers to
Early Documentation

The previous chapter is highly relevant to our study of the evidence from Ebla. The first obvious point to make is that social, legal, economic, historical, and religious documents were being written in the third millennium B.C. We have said that these tablets were copied by apprentice scribes: writing, training in the keeping of records, knowledge of other peoples' histories and traditions, study of "foreign languages", understanding of case law—it is all part of the culture of Ebla, 1,000 years before Moses. Thus, to say that originally only oral tradition was associated with the books of Moses is like saying that our 20th Century A.D. culture is less advanced than that of the 10th Century A.D. That is not an exaggeration. The time difference between 1,000 A.D. and modern times is similar to that between Ebla and Moses.

NOT ORAL TRADITION

Of course Moses wrote. Even before his time the remarkable 18th Egyptian dynasty, with its highly developed education pattern, had spread its influence far and wide. Scholars were trained in three languages, and careful recording was the order of the day. The Bible says that Moses was "learned in all the wisdom of the Egyptians", and the Documentary Hypothesis in its original form is nonsense. Writing was a common art in Moses' time. The Ebla tablets again highlight that it was an ancient art, highly developed 1,000 years before Moses' day.

Likewise, Moses' "servant", Joshua, would have been a ready scribe, especially in military and organizational matters. Aaron the priest, Moses' brother, would have been his amanuensis and consultant in priestly matters.

We must reject the Documentary Hypothesis in its emphasis on oral tradition. Such an emphasis puts the Hebrews in a category quite different from other peoples living at that time, whereas in fact they were especially ready to record the great events that uniquely marked them out as a distinctive "Covenant People". The tablets from Ebla are yet another indication that the "oral tradition" basis of the Documentary Hypothesis must be put aside.

NO SEPARATE J
OR E DOCUMENTS

We saw that the original basis (later discounted) for the Documentary Hypothesis was that there were two names for God, Jehovah (Yahweh) and Elohim. This has been shown to be fallacious from other findings, and once again the Bible has been vindicated on this point by the Ebla tablets. Actually El is the general term for God, and Yahweh is God in special covenant relationship with Israel; but even if they were two names, the evidence is clear that this was a relatively common practice in the ancient world. It was true at Ugarit, and so it was at Ebla: there was often more than one name for a particular deity. At Ugarit Baal was equated with Dagan, this being about 1,000 years after Ebla.

Such gods as Dagan, Rasaph, Sipish (later Shamash), and Ashtar all are known at Ebla. In the vocabulary lists, correspondences between various deities are shown, as with Mesopotamian and Syrian divinities. One good example is Nergal who is equated with Rasaph. Inanna is equated with Ashtar, and there are others.

The point need not be labored, for it has already been conceded by scholars around the world. The Ebla tablets, however, confirm this use of more than one name for a god much earlier than at sites such as Ugarit. If there is still objection to the earliness of the Biblical usage, we can now point to Ebla as a conclusive demonstration of such a practice.

WHAT ABOUT
THE D DOCUMENT?

I have already pointed out that there is no need to insist on a late date for the ethical teachings of Deuteronomy and the Deuteronomic school.

We also saw one especially clear example of similarity from the Ebla tablets in relation to rape. The Ebla code and that of Moses are virtually the same, as a comparison with Deuteronomy 22 makes clear. Anybody claiming that the Ebla tablets must be dated nearly 2,000 years later than the dates now accepted, would not be taken seriously. Yet that would be a parallel case to the attitude concerning the "advanced" teachings of Deuteronomy. How could Moses have been so far ahead of his contemporaries? Now it is clear that ethical teachings at a high level were known and prescribed 1,000 years before Moses.

The ethical teachings of the Bible supposedly came via the Prophets, and many scholars have traced the role of the Prophet to the seers of ancient Mari. This is another theory that they must now discount; in commenting that Ebla had a class of prophets similar to those in the Old Testament, Professor Pettinato states that

". . . to explain the Biblical phenomena scholars have hitherto looked to Mari for background, but in the future Ebla will also claim their attention."

I would take this even further. The role of the prophet is seen in the Old Testament at least as early as Genesis Chapter 9. There Noah pronounces the curse of God on Canaan (as the son on Ham), His blessing of Shem, and prophesies the "enlargement" of Japheth. Earlier, according to the Bible, God Himself spoke personally to men, but now He spoke through His servant Noah. Thus the prophet in the Biblical sense is known before Ebla, as well as before Mari.

Ebla endorses the fact that ethical prophetic writings of the Old Testament type were known long before Isaiah and the other leading prophets of Israel. Indeed, it even seems possible that Ebla itself had a "return to Yahweh" call, not unlike the challenge to holiness by the Hebrew prophets.

IL, YA, AND POLYTHEISM

About 500 gods are named in association with Ebla, so clearly it was basically a polytheistic society. However, "Il" was especially the name for "God" and had become the name for a specific god. Professor Pettinato equates this god with the "El of the Ugaritic tablets". In Ebrum's time, "Ya" also was associated with God.

He also makes the point that until the reign of Ebrum all personal names contained the theophorous element *Il* but "from Ebrum on *Il* was substituted for by *Ya*." He goes on to suggest, "It appears evident that under Ebrum a new development in West Semitic religious concepts took place that permitted the rise of *Ya*." There were certain alterations in personal names, such as Mi-ka-Il which was changed to Mi-ka-Ya; En-na-Il became En-na-Ya; Is-ra-Il is changed to Is-ra-Ya. Pettinato makes the point that this "amply demonstrates that at Ebla at least *Ya* had the same value as *Il* and points to a specific deity."

It seems to me that this is highly significant. We have seen that Ebrum's name has close affinity to the Hebrews of the Bible. Those were the people who especially knew the true God as "Ya", for that abbreviated form is seen in such names as Eli*jah*, Jerem*iah*, Obad*iah*, Zephan*iah*, and others.

This development that "permitted the rise of Ya" might well have been a time when some strong character (perhaps Ebrum himself) challenged the people to return to the concept of one true God. It does seem that they knew of such a God. That is demonstrated in the Ebla tablet of creation, where "the great one" who brought the world into being is Lugal, and this is made up of two words—originally

Lu-en-gal. "En" has religious overtones, and "Lugal" was synonymous with "the great one". It eventually came to mean "king" in Sumerian, but originally as "the great one" the word could have referred to God.

ONLY ONE GOD ON THE EBLA CREATION TABLET

This tablet associates only one God with creation. There is a close approximation to the theistic teaching of Genesis. We have already seen the dramatic differences between the Genesis record and the Babylonian *Enuma Elish* with its crude polytheism and grotesque absurdities. The Ebla tablet brings us back to a monotheism akin to that of Genesis.

I am not surprised to read of polytheism at various stages of Ebla's known history, for peoples have regularly resorted to the worship of many gods rather than accept the discipline involved in following Jehovah.

So, as I have said, I am not surprised to find that about 500 gods are named in association with Ebla. At Joshua chapter 24 Joshua gives his last great charge to the Israelite people before he himself passes on to his reward. Because of their tendency to depart from the Lord, he challenges them to make a decision: either to serve the gods in the land of the Canaanites where they were now dwelling, or to revert to the worship of the gods that their fathers worshipped on the other side of the river (the Euphrates). Joshua told them that as for him and his house, "We will serve the Lord." The people responded to his challenge and resolved that they too would serve the Lord.

Those people were quite aware of the truth of Joshua's statement that their fathers had served "other gods" before Abraham settled in Canaan. Incidentally, this reference in Joshua 24 to "the other side of the river" is another indication that Abraham's forefathers came from the southern Ur, and not the one "in the territory of Haran".

These people in Joshua's day knew that polytheism, the worship of many gods, was in their own background. Their forefathers had gone away from the worship of the one true God who was their Creator, and I am not surprised to find that many gods were worshipped at Ebla. I am also not surprised that, as previously pointed out, Professor Pettinato showed there was also a time under Ebrum when Ya was recognized, and was given a place in many personal names.

THAT SUPPOSED
P DOCUMENT

"I'm inclined to think that the P tradition is a lot of nonsense—that the Bible record is much older than has been previously admitted." So commented a well-known cuneiform scholar at the time of the revelations by the two Italian Professors.

To find this creation record at Ebla is an embarrassment to the adherents of the Documentary Hypothesis. Basically it was supposed to come from the Priestly school, dating to about the time of Ezra. This creation tablet at Ebla, dating to about 2,000 years before that time, is yet another indication that the Documentary Hypothesis is unacceptable as a basis for determining how the Old Testament documents came to us.

We quoted Professor Freedman as stating publicly that the closeness of this new tablet to Genesis Chapter 1 was somewhat of a shock. We have seen also that one other scholar expressed his surprise at "a first millennium oral Hebrew tradition" being found in a third millennium written record.

The fact is, it *is* a shock except for those who accept that this Genesis record was in writing long before Moses. The only sense in which there was a P document is that it was part of a much larger whole. There was not a series of fragments brought together after Solomon, but an original series of clay tablets that eventually found its way into the hands of Moses. He edited the components of the series and compiled them into the Book of Genesis.

THE OLD TESTAMENT
AS AUTHENTIC DOCUMENTS

Summarizing, the Ebla tablets are strong evidence against the need to have a Documentary Hypothesis to explain the development and compilation of the Old Testament documents and especially the books of Moses. Those books can be explained only as authentic records of the time claimed for them within the records themselves.

There is a creation record remarkably similar to the Genesis account. There are dealings with Hittites long before Abraham purchased the Cave of Machpelah from the Hittites of his time. It has not been long since it was argued that there were no Hittites so early. There are treaties and covenants similar to those in Exodus, and for the protection of society there are laws that point toward the concept of justice so prominent in Exodus. There are ritualistic sacrifices long before those of Leviticus, and before the Canaanites from whom some critics claimed the Hebrews borrowed them. There are prophets proclaiming their message long before the nevi'im (prophets) of the Old Testament.

By the time of the Ebla civilization these were writings that were in many ways similar to those of the books of Moses. That is not to detract from the inspiration of the Old Testament: its superiority in the realms of ethics, morality, and spiritual values stands unchallenged. The Old Testament records have that indefinable something that is different. Metaphorically, they bear within them the imprint of the finger of God.

"IT IS FORBIDDEN TO ENTER THE EXCAVATION AREAS" appears in two languages on this sign warning unauthorized visitors to keep away from the dig at the Tell Mardikh. These sentries are to assure compliance. Photo courtesy of Robert Durnal.

Chapter 10
A Concluding
Survey

The following outline is pertinent as a survey of the relevant facts.

I. THE USE OF PERSONAL NAMES
   A. Names given at a later time to Bible characters are already in use at Ebla. They include Abraham, Ishmael, Israel, Esau, Saul, Michael, and David.
   B. A list of several kings is given, including one Ebrum, which could be translated "Eber". We conclude he is NOT the Eber of Genesis 10.
   C. The city was eventually destroyed by Naram-Sin who was already known in history. This makes at least one dating point certain.

D. Cross references to other rulers such as Pepi of Egypt also give dating points. Clarification of some problems in Egyptian dating might follow.

E. A Sargon is mentioned, possibly Sargon of Akkad (the Great). Because of the scholarly conjecture that he was associated with the Tower of Babel, this might eventually be of interest in the study of Bible backgrounds.

We consider the change of personal names, from "Il" to "Ya", under V. OTHER RELIGIOUS CONCEPTS.

II. BIBLE CITIES REFERRED TO BY NAME

A. The tablets include the earliest known reference to Jerusalem.

B. A city called "Salim" is also mentioned, and it is possible that this is the "Salem" over which Melchizedek was king.

C. Sodom and Gomorrah and the other three "cities of the plain" (referred to at Genesis 14:2) are known as trading centers.

D. A city called Ur is referred to, "in the territory of Haran." We analyze the evidence and conclude that this was not the Biblical city of Ur, from which

Abraham came. In fact, clues in the Bible clarify the issue, suggesting that the fact of two cities with the same name was known.

E. The tablets include many references to trading centers, and a number of cities known later in the Bible are mentioned. These include Dor, Hazor, Megiddo, Lachish, Gaza, Sinai, Ashtaroth, Joppa, and Haran. Isaiah refers to Carchemish by its ancient name.

III. EARLY REFERENCES TO PEOPLES/EMPIRES

A. The Sumerians are well-known by cultural, trade, and linguistic ties.

B. The Amorites are also well-attested, being more established than had been previously known.

C. The city of Ebla was the center of a vast and prosperous empire. It is of far greater importance than modern scholars had suspected. Many ancient history textbooks will need re-writing.

D. People such as the Hittites and Canaanites are mentioned in the tablets. Professor Pettinato has labelled the language of Ebla "Paleo-Canaanite".

E. The name of the king "Eber" [Ebrum] appears to have a linguistic tie with the word "Hebrew". The language is at times remarkably close to Hebrew.

IV. THE RELEVANCE TO THE "DOCUMENTARY HYPOTHESIS"

A. Gods of different nations are equated, examples being Nergash/Rasaph and Inanna/Ishtar. The supposed use of two names for God (J for Jehovah/Yahweh, and E for Elohim) was the original basis for the Documentary Hypothesis. The Ebla findings are a further demonstration of that foundation being false.

B. The "D" Document, centuries after Moses, is yet another concept that must be put aside. Ebla laws dealing with sexual offenses are remarkably close to passages such as Deuteronomy 22:22-30.

C. The role of the prophet is much earlier than the "Documentary Hypothesis" allowed. One of the conclusions from Ebla is that the office of prophet must now be dated prior to Mari: the Old Testament traces it to at least Noah. The ethical teachings of

Moses are perfectly acceptable and need not be pushed on to a much later period, as the Documentary Hypothesis insisted.

D. The law-code at Ebla is the oldest yet found at an ancient site. The Documentary Hypothesis originally postulated that law codes were unknown in Moses' time, but a number predating Moses are now known. At Ebla there are tablets dealing with judicial proceedings, and there is elaborate discussion of case law.

E. The need for a "P" ("Priestly") Document is likewise rejected. It supposedly included the record of creation, eventually brought into the Canon at some time after the exile. Now it is accepted that a somewhat similar account must be dated to approximately 2,000 years earlier than that time. The "oral tradition" apparently was in written form after all.

V. OTHER RELIGIOUS CONCEPTS

A. Only one Supreme Being is associated with the record of Creation. It is also interesting (in a trade tablet) that the place "Dilmun" is named. This was already known on a "paradise" epic, but it was not usually thought of as an actual place.

B. Mesopotamian deities of a later time are now known at Ebla, including Enki, Enlil, Utu, Inanna, Tiamut, Marduk, and Nada. The Flood tablet is more like the Babylonian account than that of the Bible.

C. Point (B) above illustrated the polytheism that was common at Ebla at some stages of her history. In fact, 500 gods are known in her background. Although one God (or "Great One"—a word that came to mean "King") was known in Creation, there was clearly a decline to polytheism.

D. Although Il (El in later times) was a general term for "god", it was also the name of a particular god. Many people of Ebla showed their great respect for this god by including his name in the names of their children.

E. At one time in the history of Ebla, the name of El in people's names was replaced by Ya. This pointed to the acceptance of "Ya" instead of "Il". "Ya" is the ending in such names in the

Bible as Isaiah, Jeremiah, Nehemiah, Elijah, and Beniah. That "one time" in Ebla's history was just the time when Eber (Ebrum) was king. Thus the recognition of Yahweh in a new way is very possibly linked with the people who had ethnic associations with the people later known in the Bible as Hebrews.

The story has only just begun. There will be echoes from Ebla for generations to come, and it is probable that a great deal more light will be thrown on Bible backgrounds as a result.

It is at least thought-provoking that findings such as those at Ebla consistently support the Bible as a thoroughly acceptable record. To me it is far more than a wonderful history text: it is God's Word of Truth, His revelation of Himself in the Person of His Son.

Appendix

Ebla-An Update

As this book goes into its third printing it is appropriate to do what we can to bring the subject up to date.

The importance of Ebla was great indeed in the third millennium B.C., with some of its inhabitants trading far and wide. Ebla's economic activities extended to Beirut, Byblos, Damascus, Mari, Kish, and Ashur. There was even some contact with Egypt. Previously Syria was regarded as a mere buffer state between Sumer and Egypt, but it has become clear that Syria itself was an economic giant.

The tablets also make clear that the world was much more populous than was thought a decade ago. Over 5,000 different geographic regions are mentioned on the first 20,000 tablets recovered, and this indicates that during the third millennium B.C. traders journeyed across lands that were relatively well populated. Ebla itself was surrounded by a large number of small states. It is somewhat of a surprise to find there was a highly developed urban civilization as early as 2300 B.C.

WHEN DID ABRAHAM LIVE?

This has led to some surprising conclusions. Muslims believe that Abraham journeyed around the Middle East about 2300 B.C., and some scholars are suggesting that they were right. Included in their number is Professor David Noel Freedman of the University of Michigan. In a 1978 address entitled "Archaeology and Biblical Religion", delivered at Pittsburgh Theological Seminary, Professor Freedman is recorded as making some highly relevant comments.

He specifically rejects the view of two scholars, John Van Seters and Thomas L. Thompson, who argue that Genesis 14 is not an account relating to a patriarchal experience in the second millennium B.C., but is the product of the first millennium B.C. Freedman concedes that the Biblical editors might have utilized the story because it had analogies between the days of its happening and current events, but then he says, "But it is going much too far to say that these same people invented the story in order to make their point; no, they obviously believed that it was an authentic record of the past, peculiarly fitting to be preserved and transmitted to the present generation and for posterity, but certainly not a fiction devised for this purpose."

Freedman goes on to give his own opinion following the findings of the Ebla Tablets, and especially regarding the references to the "Cities of the Plain," including Sodom and Gomorrah. Professor Freedman states, "It is now my belief that the story in Genesis 14 not only corresponds in content to the Ebla Tablet, but that the Genesis account derives from the same period." He suggests that scholars have been looking in the wrong millennium for the correct historical location of this story. He states, "Briefly put, the account in Genesis 14, and also in Chapters 18-19, does not belong to the second millennium B.C., still less to the first millennium B.C., but rather to the third millennium B.C."

THE EBLA REFERENCE TO SODOM & GOMORRAH

Freedman goes on to acknowledge that he is making a large claim, "and the few people brave or foolhardy enough to follow this lead, are the only ones to make it." He then discusses the important relationship of the Sodom and Gomorrah data. He tells of a conversation with Professor Pettinato in which it was made clear that the five Cities of the Plain, as listed in Genesis 14, were referred to in one Ebla tablet.

In passing, we notice that Professor Pettinato has later stated that the Cities were not referred to on one tablet but spread over two tablets. We are not in a position to insist that it was one tablet or two, but it is highly relevant to mention that Professor Freedman tells of a remarkable conversation that he had with Professor Pettinato dealing with these tablets, and even the fact that the name of the king of one of the cities was mentioned. Professor Freedman's own excitement about the matter is made clear in the address referred to above.

We are not dealing only with the names of cities, however. What follows is a personal account of an extraordinary experience, certainly the most unusual in my career as a scholar. It involved only Professor Pettinato and me, at breakfast in the Quadrangle Club at the University of Chicago, on 5 November 1976; we were traveling together to major universities in the midwest and the east, so that he could present information about the Ebla tablets and discuss his findings with Sumerologists and historians. During breakfast we were talking about the tablet with the names of the five cities of the plain on it, and which he had described publicly a few days earlier at the meetings in St. Louis. I asked him whether there were any additional details about the cities or their kings which he could divulge. Since he did not have a transcript of the tablet, or even a picture of it with him, he had to work from memory, and could not remember all the details since the tablet was a large one and contained hundreds of city-names along with the information about the individual commercial transactions between Ebla and the other cities. After some cogitation, he informed me that he could remember the name of one of the kings of the cities of the plain on the Ebla tablet.

As we consider the above statements, made verbally by Professor Freedman at that time, it is clear that the two scholars were on good terms—traveling together, eating breakfast together, discussing "the tablet with the names of the five cities of the plain on it." It is also clear that Professor Pettinato "had described publicly a few days earlier" this same tablet.

It is relevant to comment I had the privilege, as shown earlier in this book, of meeting privately with the archaeologist, the epigrapher, several other scholars, and Professor Freedman at a private dinner. Certainly Professor Pettinato was on terms of friendship with Professor Freedman, and Professor Matthiae was also. The criticisms against Professor Freedman that have since appeared certainly were not in keeping with the spirit of warmth and scholarly cordiality that were evident at that time.

We shall see that there have been objections by the Syrian people as to the relevance made to the Bible, and both Pettinato and Matthiae have publicly disclaimed much of Professor Freedman's enthusiastic association with the Bible. At the time when I was in their company, there certainly was no such dissociation. One wonders if political expediency has forced the hands of the two Italian archaeologists. We shall necessarily refer to that again.

WERE THERE TWO KINGS
NAMED "BIRSHA"?

Our interest at the moment is merely to make the point that Professor Freedman has come to the place where he suggests that Abraham must be dated in the 23rd Century B.C. He tells how, in that breakfast meeting, Professor Pettinato wrote down the name of a king which was the same as "Birsha," the king of Gomorrah referred to in Genesis 14. Freedman also tells us that Pettinato later found that the king mentioned on the Ebla tablet was king of the city of Admah, whereas in Genesis 14 Birsha is king of Gomorrah. Professor Pettinato was working from memory, and at that time Dr. Freedman suggested that they should work in a properly scientific manner, with Pettinato writing down the name of the king before he himself saw a copy of the Hebrew text. Only then should they compare the two names: "I suggested to Pettinato that we should proceed in a strictly scientific way, and that he should write down the name which he recalled from the tablet in an appropriate syllabic transcription before we discussed the information from the Bible. In that way we would be assured that his transcription would not be influenced in any possible way by knowledge of the biblical names."

Pettinato agreed to this, and wrote down the name according to his best judgment, concealed what he had written, and Professor Freedman obtained a Hebrew Bible from Professor Gelb at the Oriental Institute. The name that Professor Pettinato had written down was bi-ir-ša. (This form of "s" = "sh".) In the Biblical account, the name of the king of Gomorrah is given as Birsha. As I said above, it later turned out that in the Ebla tablet Birsha was said to be the king of Admah, whereas in the Genesis 14 account Birsha is king of Gomorrah.

This could mean that there were two men with the same name, possibly it being a popular name at the time, and that is a common phenomenon. Another possibility is that these kings were roughly contemporary, but not exactly so. In any case, as Freedman himself points out, the Ebla tablet was written while the towns were thriving, whereas the Biblical account is dealing with the time when they were actually destroyed. Freedman suggests that perhaps the Ebla tablet was 50 or even 100 years earlier than the Biblical record, but that both were within the Early Bronze Age.

Freedman suggests another possibility—that the names were recorded in the Bible in a mnemonic pattern as a way of facilitating the preservation and transmission of the data.

My suggestion is slightly different. As we look at the association of the group of kings in Genesis 14, we find there are actually two groups, and in the second group Gomorrah and Admah are linked. If the Biblical account is slightly later than the Ebla account,

131

as Freedman suggests, it is possible that there was some family connection between the rulers of Gomorrah and Admah.

"AN ASTOUNDING MOMENT"

Freedman discusses the way in which the Biblical names have been preserved. He states, "Beginning with the biblical form we would get the Eblaite spelling; but beginning with the Ebla form, we would not necessarily arrive at the biblical spelling. In fact the biblical form of the name is quite distinctive if not unique, since quadriliteral nouns (roots with four consonants) are quite rare in Semitic, and this one cannot now be duplicated from any source . . . . While the name of the king, Birsha, is the most striking single example of extraordinary fidelity to tradition, there are many others when we compare the forms in the Ebla tablets with those in the Bible."

For Professor Freedman this was "an astounding moment." He suggests that the evidence is strong that the tablet and the Biblical record must belong to the same chronological horizon: "With eight names the same in both documents, including especially the name of a person, the correlation must be temporal as well as verbal . . . . "

As to the use of the name "Birsha," Professor Freedman suggests that the answer is that there is a mnemonic pattern associated with the names of the cities and their kings, with the rather similar names Bera and Birsha linked together as kings of Sodom and Gomorrah and with Shinab and Shemeber brought together as the kings of the other paired cities Admah and Zeboiim. Freedman suggests that the Biblical arrangement "helped to preserve all the names correctly, but not necessarily the political realities. It may be that in the course of oral transmission, the names were accidentally or deliberately grouped in the fashion in which they are recorded in order to facilitate memory."

I happen not to accept Professor Freedman's argument, but it is put forward as a matter of factual reporting. Possibly the answer is better contained in Freedman's own alternative suggestion as follows:

> We do not say, therefore, that Birsha of the tablet is the same person as Birsha of the Genesis narrative. We suggest strongly however that if they are not the same person, they belong to the same era, quite possibly to the same dynasty or to related families. We can go further now and argue that the tradition in Genesis 14 reflects conditions in the Near East that also are reflected in the Ebla tablets: the pre-Sargonic Early Dynastic era in Mesopotamia and Syria-Palestine.

He further suggests that this was before the emergence of the empire of Sargon the Great and the First Dynasty of Akkad. He says, "Just as the Ebla tablets reflect the situation prior to that development, so also does Genesis 14." He makes the additional point that the archaeological evidence for the levels of occupation in the relevant region of the Dead Sea would support this argument. He points out that the evidence suggests that the Cities of the Plain, if properly identified by excavators, such as the late Paul Lapp and Nancy Lapp of Pittsburgh Theological Seminary, and more recently by Thomas Schaub and Walter Rast, indicate that there was occupation in the Early Bronze Age, but there was not occupation in the Middle Bronze Age. It follows that if the Cities of the Plain were destroyed in the time of Abraham, as recorded in the Bible, then Abraham must have lived in the Early Bronze Age and not in the Middle Bronze Age.

THE NEW DISCOVERIES
ARE DISTURBING

One comment is relevant at this point. As a conservative, it is, of course, delightful to read a scholar such as Freedman coming out so positively for the early date of the Biblical record. Note this statement by Professor Freedman:

> The implications of the new discoveries for a reconsideration and reconstruction of patriarchal history are profound and to a considerable degree disturbing. Under any circumstances, they

should not leave anyone in a complacent mood, since no existing blueprint or plan is viable. Conservatives may take some comfort from the apparent vindication of biblical tradition, where it can be checked. Liberals can console themselves that if a newer and truer picture of biblical origins has been attained, it has been through the vigorous use of scientific historical, archaeological, and linguistic methods, and not derived dogmatically from prior commitments, theological and otherwise.

Remember that Professor Freedman is the editor of *The Biblical Archaeologist* and is recognized as a leading scholar in the realm of Biblical archaeology. He is a Jewish scholar, not a Christian, and certainly would not identify himself with so-called fundamentalist views of the Bible, even with regard to the Old Testament, much less the New Testament. It is remarkable to read such a scholar using the word "profound" as to the implications of this patriarchal period of Biblical history.

PETTINATO REFERRED TO *ONE* TABLET

It should be noticed that it was Professor Pettinato himself who announced that the references to the five Cities of the Plain were found on one tablet. It was he who made this announcement at the annual meeting of various learned societies, such as the Society of Biblical Literature and the American Schools of Oriental Research, at St. Louis on October 29, 1976. He did not only announce that he had found the names of the five Cities of the Plain but also that they were in the same order as they were found in the Bible, at Genesis Chapter 14.

In earlier days of this century that record in Genesis 14 was severely criticized by many scholars. However, the researchers of Nelson Glueck, together with others such as W. F. Albright, eventually made it clear that there was a line of cities along the line of a trade route as would fit the Biblical record. Instead of it being thought as a legendary story, the chapter became accepted as a remarkably accurate and factual account.

ONE CITY WITH TWO NAMES

The second tablet clears up why the one city would have two names at the one time, as is implied in the Biblical record. Again we quote from Professor Freedman: "It states that Zoar is a town within the district of Bela, which constitutes the larger urban complex. That was the situation in the era of Ebla, and apparently the Biblical record reflects that circumstance without specifying the details."

Freedman makes the point that not only are the names the same when systems of writing are taken into account, but the order is the same as well. As he points out, it is a correlation of five for five, and even six for six when the second name of Bela for Zoar is taken into account.

We are not insisting that Professor Freedman is right as to that early date for Abraham, but the arguments he put forward should be taken seriously. If the genealogical lists of Genesis are complete, without any gaps, then it is hard to see how Freedman's early date could be accepted. If, however, there are gaps, especially in the genealogical lists *after* Abraham, then it would indeed be possible to accept such an early date for Abraham. One interesting point is that this could throw light on other problem dates, such as the long debated issue as to how long Abraham's descendants were in Egypt before the Exodus.

A comparison of I Chronicles 3:11,12 with Matthew 1:8,9 shows that Matthew omitted Joash, Amaziah, and Azariah. Some scholars attribute this to literary style and point out that terms such as "son of" and "begat" can mean "in the same direct line." For whatever reason, they were omitted and on such an argument Abraham's date could be pushed back into the third millennium B.C.

Perhaps the strongest argument for the correlation of the patriarchal period with Ebla is that the site of Bab edh-Dhra was apparently finally destroyed and abandoned about 2250 B.C., in EB IV. Bad edh-Dhra is now believed to have been one of the Cities of the Plain, and none of them had any sign of Middle Bronze Age settlement.

All this is startling in its implications. If indeed these are the Cities of the Plain, and we are to insist on the accuracy of the Biblical record, and if the identification of early Bronze pottery, etc., is correct, then we must recognize that Abraham was alive at this same time. Genesis 19 clearly establishes that he saw the smoke of the destruction from where he stood near Hebron.

Freedman also makes the point that the city of Damascus is mentioned in Genesis 19 and also on the same Ebla tablet that mentions the five Cities of the Plain. He does not make a great deal of this, but suggests it is yet another indirect confirmation of the obviously correct Biblical association.

LET'S NOT JUMP TO CONCLUSIONS

Freedman's case is thought provoking and cannot be lightly dismissed. However, it also should not be swiftly accepted in its totality. There are three points that make it unnecessary to be swayed to a swift conclusion that Abraham was virtually contemporary with the collapse of Ebla at the hands of Naram-Sin. They are:

1. There has been considerable debate over the last 25 years as to the date to be ascribed to Bab edh-Dhra's final phase. Dates have fluctuated by more than 200 years.

2. The date of the final occupation level of these five cities (probably correctly identified as the Biblical "Cities of the

Plain") is not certainly established as contemporary with Ebla's destruction by Naram-Sin. Those cities were far enough away from the major trade routes for changes (e.g. in pottery styles) to be much slower than in a major commercial and world center such as Ebla.

3. In any case, there is considerable challenge to some aspects of both Early and Middle Bronze Age dating. These "Ages" have not been established with sufficient precision to demand a re-dating for Abraham.

In any case, the cities could well have been thriving long after Ebla's collapse. The use of the name "Birsha" for one of the kings might be no more a coincidence than that the name "Abraham" is known both at Ebla and in the Bible.

We recognize that some Christian scholars hold to an earlier date for Abraham than is traditionally accepted. This is based on the theory that some periods of human (Hebrew) history are not counted in the divine record, because the people were out of the will of God. The major example often used is the wilderness journey under Moses.

The argument is interesting, and according to some writers it would bring the date of Abraham well into the third millennium. The theory is mentioned in passing and not necessarily dismissed. There are areas of spiritual reality where all of us are as children. Perhaps this is one of them. However, at present I do not hold to a third millennium date for Abraham.

THE ASSYRIAN KING LIST—
AND BIBLE PEOPLE

Another point with Biblical overtones relates to the famous Assyrian King List, dating back to the times when the kings lived in tents. The first name is of Tudiya, King of Assur, this being the name of the Assyrian priestly center and their god. Our modern word Assyria comes from it. This king turns up in the list at Ebla, having entered into a treaty with the King of Ebla. This clearly demonstrates his historicity.

Professor Freedman makes the point that the Biblical figures are also centered in history. He does not suggest that the record was put into writing at the time accepted by conservative scholars, but that the men themselves were real figures. He says, "Nevertheless, behind the symbolic figures preserved in second millennium traditions, there are real people of the third millennium. As in the case of Tudiya of Assur, whose symbolic importance in the long list of kings of Assyria cannot be doubted, it is clear now that he was a real, not an invented, historical figure."

Freedman relates this concept of symbolic figures to Abraham and says, "Behind the symbolic figure of the second millennium and later speculation and reverence, there is a real man, a human being of the third millennium." He argues that Abraham remains identifiable as a real person more than

140

ever before.

At the beginning of his address, Freedman had made the point that the Ebla tablets generally "confirm or at least support the basic positions maintained by giants like Albright and Speiser, while effectively undercutting the prevailing skepticism and sophistry of the larger contingent representative of Continental and American scholarship."

KENNETH KITCHEN COMMENTS

Kenneth Kitchen takes the argument even further. In *The Bible and Its World* he points out that until 1975 this shadowy name that heads the Assyrian list (which itself was comprised about 1000 B.C. in its first form) had been treated with great skepticism. People even referred to it as a free invention or a corruption. As Kitchen says:

> Whereas in fact, the name is real, the man is real, he was indeed Assyrian king as the List records, and as such signed a treaty with Ebrum, king of Ebla. Thus, the genealogical tradition of the early part of the Assyrian King List (linked as it is with Hammurabi's ancestral line back from c. 1650 B.C.) is to this extent vindicated as preserving faithfully the memory of real early people who were Assyrian rulers. Not dissimilar material in the Old Testament, therefore, such as genealogical

material in Genesis II or patriarchal traditions, should be
treated with similar respect. (pp.
48-49)

Kitchen does a great deal to show that
earlier criticisms relating to the organization
of the cults, sacrifices, rituals, etc., were
wrong in their claims that such practices
were not known until a much later time. He
states that well-organized temple rituals were
known in all historic times.

They have nothing to do with
baseless theories of the 19th century AD, whereby such features of
religious life can only be a mark of
"late sophistication," virtually
forbidden to the Hebrews until
after the Babylonian exile—alone
of all the peoples of the ancient
East. (p. 54)

The rites associated with Moses' taber-
nacle (and with Solomon's temple) were
known in their times after all and were not
merely the invention of writers living in the
fifth century B.C.

Another point that Freedman makes is
that if other heads of groups would keep
records such as those of Ebla, it is likely
that Abraham also would keep some sort of
record of various business transactions and
files of necessary communications. Abraham
would not have had the same need for files
as the kings of Genesis 14 and 19, but there
is no reason to suggest that he would not
have kept records of some of his quite

elaborate transactions.

ABRAHAM CAME FROM UR
IN THE SOUTH

Another relevant point from the *National Geographic* article of December, 1978, is the reference to records from Ur of the Chaldees that mention two Eblaites by name—Ili-Dagan and Gura. We read also of "Surin, the messenger, the man from Ebla," who had made votive offerings to the local god.

Ur of the Chaldees is thus shown to be in relationship with Ebla to the north. Ur here is the Ur that was excavated by Sir Leonard Woolley, and again we stress the point made earlier in this book that there were two Urs. Some critics have argued that, because the Ebla tablets refer to "Ur in the territory of Haran," this means the northern Ur. We have discussed this earlier, and when we look at the record of Abraham leaving Ur to go to Haran, in the speech of Stephen recorded at Acts Chapter 7, it is clear that Abraham is not just going from one suburb to another, but from one country to another. He is clearly told to depart from his country and to go into the land that is to be shown to him. Abraham obeyed and went out from the land of the Chaldeans. The reason the Bible writer refers to Ur of the Chaldees is probably to make it clear that it was the southern city, and not the northern city. There are many cases in ancient history (and in modern history, too) where there is more than one city with the same name. "Of the Chaldees" was a later editing note, we suggest, to make it clear that Abraham's city of Ur was the southern one—*not* the northern one near Haran.

A further point of interest, confirmed by the Bible reference in Isaiah, comes from the records of Sargon. We learn that he sent his troops against Ashdod and besieged and conquered it and then plundered the city. Something rather similar to this Assyrian writing is found from the records of a high Army official from Ebla who tells us, "The town of Aburu and the town of Ilgi . . . . I besieged and I conquered . . . . piles of corpses I gathered in the land." (Quoted in *National Geographic*, December, 1978, p. 855.) This was in a letter from the general to his king. The boasting of those two kings, separated by hundreds of years, was remarkably similar!

WHAT IS THE RELEVANCE OF EBLA TO THE BIBLE?

After the initial claims that the Ebla tablets were highly relevant for early Bible records, there has been a chorus of voices raised to suggest that there should be more caution. It is entirely possible that this is more politic than scholarly as such, and Professor Freedman has been the subject of attack as to his supposed overreadiness to relate the finds to the early Bible records.

However, as Professor Freedman himself said in the Pittsburgh address mentioned previously, "In this situation, the danger may lie in the opposite direction: in the general stampede to look wise and be discreet, a really significant piece of information may be overlooked, and there will be silence when circumstances call for boldness and loudness, even showmanship."

In view of the outcry against Biblical relevance and association, we consider some of the specific criticisms.

The *Aramco World Magazine* of March-April, 1978, is especially dealing with the Ebla finds. It is an issue called "Ebla: City of the White Stones." At page 18 Professor Matthiae is quoted as saying, "Another thing is that the international press has sometimes followed the lines of non-existing relations between Ebla and the Bible, thus forgetting the real importance of the discovery . . . . But, as some important newspapers underlined clearly, the real importance is *historical*." He goes on to make the point, "For the first time, we know a properly Syrian culture existed in the third millennium" (p. 18). He further states, "We now have the beginning of a real great revolution in our work and studies" (p. 18).

There is certainly an attempt by the Italians to minimize the relevance of these texts to the Hebrew and Christian Scriptures. In *National Geographic* of December, 1978, Professor Matthiae states, "In my opinion, the claimed Biblical associations are not based on real evidence; the divine name Yahweh does not appear at all in

Ebla texts . . . . ''

However, this is at variance with the claims of the epigrapher, Professor Giovanni Pettinato, who claimed that it seemed probable that names with the form ''El'' had been changed to have the form ''Yah''— one example he gave was of the name Mi-ka-il (Who is like God?) being changed to Mi-ka-ya (Who is like Ya?). This is elaborated by Reverend Mitchell Dahood, Dean of the Pontifical Biblical Institute's Oriental Faculty in Rome, in that same *National Geographic* article, at pages 737-740.

POLITICAL ASPECT?

Another relevant report is in *Biblical Archaeology Review,* September/October, 1978, at pages 2, 3, 4, and 6. A writer taking the pseudonym of Adam Mikaya writes to suggest that there is a political side to the story. According to ''Adam Mikaya,'' ''This political aspect makes everyone connected with Ebla vulnerable, so this report—and possibly subsequent reports—will have to be written pseudonymously.'' Mikaya makes the well-known point that anyone living in academia is living in a political jungle, and Ebla is no exception. He makes the point that Paolo Matthiae and Giovanni Pettinato were literally not speaking to each other for several months. He tells of Pettinato being barred from the dig by Matthiae, as well as from the museum in Aleppo in Syria where there are crates of cuneiform tablets stored.

Apart from Old Testament associations,

one point of disagreement between the scholars relates to the dating, with Matthiae saying that they date from 2400 to 2250 B.C., whereas Pettinato puts forward the dates of 2580 to 2450 B.C. The finding of references to Pepi I and to Kephren of Egypt are highly relevant and seem to support the dates given by Matthiae. This is an important point, for if Pettinato is right, it might even mean that the archaeologists as such have missed a stratum at Ebla.

Another troublesome issue was that Pettinato was the man to whom most people wanted to talk, because he had translated some of the tablets; whereas Matthiae was the one who had labored for many years in the relative obscurity of unexciting field work—until the tablets were found. There is considerable friction between the men, and as the article in BAR makes clear, "Matthiae became understandably upset when everyone wanted to talk to Pettinato, not him . . . . After ten years of work, Matthiae watched as Pettinato reaped the glory."

A further issue was the actual publication of the information in the texts. Matthiae had found them, but he could not read them, and Matthiae actually appointed a ten-man committee to direct the translation and then the publication of the tablets. Pettinato would not work with this group at first. He later changed his mind after the President of Italy, so it is reported, called the two men in and insisted that they make up the feud.

However, it seems that the biggest problem is in regard to the emphasis that has been made on the Bible. "The Syrian government, however, would like to play down, if not suppress this aspect of the tablets." (BAR, p. 3.) The article points out that this is not new in Arab countries, as American archaeologists working in Jordan know that they must tread lightly in reporting Iron Age finds lest they anger local archaeological and government personnel. It goes on to say, "The situation in Syria is worse. If Matthiae wishes to stay in the good graces of his Syrian hosts, he will not be emphasizing the Biblical implications of his finds. Rather he will be talking about Syrian history during the Bronze Age" (p. 3).

"HOGWASH!" SAYS
PROFESSOR BUCCELLATI

In fairness to the parties concerned, it should be stated that in that same issue of BAR the idea of politics being involved is rejected by Professor Buccellati, a highly reputable American scholar now helping with the translation of the Ebla tablets. His article is headed by the word "Hogwash." Professor Buccellati is quoted as saying, "Anyone making such a suggestion is either showing his gross ignorance or is guilty of bad faith." It is pointed out that Buccellati is the only American-based scholar on the ten-man translation team. Professor Buccellati makes the point that other centers such as Ugarit and Mari are also in Syria, and that these have been extremely important in Biblical studies but that the Syrians have never expressed concern over them.

However, there is a difference. Those two sites were excavated at a time when tension between Syria and Israel was not as high as it is today. Wars and rumors of war have caused it to be quite clear that there is indeed intense jealousy and bitterness, and, for whatever reason, it is clear that the two Italian Professors have changed their approach as to their preparedness to be identified with the Bible as the fruits of their excavations are made more public.

Matthiae and Pettinato have joined forces. They declare that there has been exaggeration of the impact on the Bible, and that basically these tablets are demonstrating the greatness of a former Syrian empire. In this new approach, Professor David Noel Freedman is severely criticized. As this BAR article says, "But Freedman is himself now *persona non grata* at Ebla and in Syria, although it was he who first brought Matthiae and Pettinato to worldwide attention and popularized the Ebla tablets in the United States." That review points out that the Arabic press in Damascus has been critical of Professor Freedman because of the way he has emphasized the Biblical connections of the tablets. Matthiae has claimed that Freedman has emphasized the Biblical aspects because his own public image is thereby enhanced. Certain it is that Matthiae and Pettinato are going out of their way to deny that the Ebla tablets are as relevant to the Old Testament as has been claimed.

It has already been shown in this book that in the early days of reporting the finds, Matthiae and Pettinato were both quite happy to participate in the presentation associated with Professor Freedman, as large crowds at various United States centers could testify.

A DAMASCUS INTERVIEW

I have a photocopy of an interview in a Damascus journal called *Flash*. My copy is undated, but comes from a properly printed journal, and it is in English. It is headed "New Facts About Ebla," and is supposedly an interview with Professor Giovanni Pettinato of the University of Rome. This itself is a basic error, for the interview is actually with Professor Paolo Matthiae. Matthiae refers to himself, and also to Professor Pettinato, in ways that make it quite clear that it is in fact Matthiae who is being interviewed.

The article claims that the one being interviewed is refuting "all Zionist allegations aimed at defacing the Syrian Arab history" (p. 20). One question by the interviewer (on page 21) is as follows:

> Some newspapers have specified that David Noel Freedman takes part in your mission. Who is this man, and what is his relationship

with the mission? What would you do if his pretension were a slander?

In answer to this Professor Matthiae is quoted as stating:

Mr. Freedman has never taken part in our mission and I do most clearly specify that the Archaeological Mission of Rome University in Syria, which I am at the head of since its foundation in 1964, has been exclusively composed of Italian members. Mr. Freedman has no relation with the Italian Mission.

The article is insulting to Professor Freedman, such as this statement in a question:

Freedman pretends to have met you in Rome in June 1976.

Professor Matthiae minimizes this by answering that he has met, and he does meet, dozens of colleagues and scholars. He goes on to acknowledge that he had met Mr. Freedman in Rome. There is no pretending whatever, as the facts make clear, that Freedman had in fact met Professor Matthiae. Professor Freedman had of course made this clear in his earlier factual reports.

The questioner goes on to state that Professor Freedman is supposedly a member of a Confederacy which is involved with the Masonic Jewish brotherhood known as B'Nai Brith, and the questioner says to Matthiae, "Have you realized later on the serious role assigned to Freedman to falsify the truth and to give deceptive interpretations? (p. 21)." Professor Matthiae states in answer that he is not aware of Mr. Freedman's political ideas, nor of his contingent part in equivocal political associations.

Professor Matthiae also states certain things about Dr. Pettinato. He says:

> Mr. Pettinato is a specialist of the Sumerian and the Akkadian, and of the languages of Mesopotamia which are written in Cuneiform, in general. The intentions of Mr. Pettinato in his interpretations of the tablets of Ebla is a matter relating to my conscience as a scholar and man. I can only tell you that I most vividly deplore the unscientific valuations decided upon without the necessary ripe reflection. I also have to specify that the declarations given by Mr. Pettinato were neither authorized nor approved by me, and they in no way reflect the interpretations of the Italian Mission, but they are only his personal ideas.

As he draws his article to a close Professor Matthiae gives a strong vote of thanks to the Syrian Arab Republic authorities, and says that between the Directorate of Antiquities and the Italian Mission "there has always and for thirteen years been the most intimate and the fruitful collaboration." He passes on a vote of thanks to specific individuals among the Syrian authorities.

"GENESIS CHAPTER 1" —
AND CREATION

I believe that Professor Freedman has been made something of a scapegoat in all this. It was Freedman who arranged a lecture tour for these two Italian Professors, and it was obvious that there were cordial public relations toward Professor Freedman. I personally asked for information about the Creation and Flood tablets, and Professor Freedman, chairing the luncheon at which the question was asked, shrugged his shoulders and suggested that I ask Pettinato for the answer. I did just that, and at that dinner table Professor Pettinato thought for a moment, then said, "Genesis Chapter 1." There was a surprised silence for a moment, and then the scholars around that table asked questions as to the relevance of Genesis Chapter 1. Professor Pettinato was very specific that the tablet that had been found was closer to Genesis Chapter 1 than any other yet known.

Then, and in the discussions that followed—public as well as private—he quite clearly saw links with the Ebla tablets and factual records of the Bible. One important example is the way he recognized close relationships between the "Paleo-Canaanite" of Ebla and the early Hebrew language.

This type of association with the Bible was not evident only at that rather select-company dinner. At the public meetings afterward it was clear that there was a recognition of considerable association with Biblical backgrounds, along the lines that have been made clear previously in this book.

In addition, Professor Freedman is the editor of the prestigious journal, *Biblical Archaeologist.* Its editorial committee consists of Frank M. Cross, Edward F. Campbell, Jr., William G. Dever, John S. Holladay, Jr., and H. Darrell Lance. Both the Italian Professors have contributed extensive articles to *Biblical Archaeologist.* In the May, 1976, edition, there is an extensive article by Professor Pettinato. It is not our purpose at this stage to reanalyze that article, but here is one quotation:

> Among these kings the most interesting, also for his Biblical reminiscences, is surely Ebrum, whose name is written Eb-uru-um, with two possible readings: Eb-ru-um whose resemblance to Eber, the father of the Semites according to Gen. 10:21, is truly surprising, or Eb-ri-um, which inevitably elicits *ibri,* "Hebrew." Of the two possibilities, I would choose the second (p. 47).

DOES EBLA REFER TO JEHOVAH?

Another highly important point is the identification of the Hebrew god Yahweh (Jehovah). Pettinato discusses this and tells us:

> The term *Il* doubtless indicates "god" in general, but also a specific divinity, the god Il/El of the Ugaritic tablets. Ya is still considered a *crux interpretum* so far as it could be rather understood as a hypocoristicon, i.e., a shortened form. But the alternation in the personal names such as Mi-ka-Il/Mi-ka-Ya, En-na-Il/En-na-Ya, Is-ra-Il/Is-ra-Ya amply demonstrates that at Ebla at least Ya had the same value as Il and points to a specific deity. Now the new fact revealed by the Ebla tablets is this: while till the reign of Ebrum all personal names contained the theophorous element Il, from Ebrum on Il was substituted for by Ya. Here I merely note the fact, but it appears evident that under Ebrum a new development in West Semitic religious concepts took place that permitted the rise of Ya (p. 48).

If this be the sort of Biblical association of which Pettinato is "guilty," it is interesting to note that he is not alone in his conclusion. In the BAR article mentioned before it is reported that the argument over the use of the determinative "Ya" has now been brought to a head by a tablet at Ebla, spelled with the divine determinative. The name is semantically equivalent to the Hebrew name

"Yoram," which means, "Ya is exalted." The claim goes on to say that Ya or Yahweh was therefore known at Ebla at some time in the third millennium B.C. The actual name, as reported, is "Ya-ra-mu." "The name is Ya-ra-mu which is preceded by the divine determinative, signifying that Ya is a divine element."

A STRICTLY ARCHAEOLOGICAL APPROACH?

Professor Matthiae's article is not so specific as to any direct or indirect association with the Old Testament, for he writes as an archaeologist telling what buildings, etc., were found, rather than as a translator of tablets. He outlines the reasons why the tell was excavated and gives fascinating accounts of how the audience court and so much more were recovered. He recounts how the first 40 cuneiform economic tablets were discovered on the floor in one of the long rooms and gives exciting facts as other rooms were found which also contained tablets. He tells us:

In 1975 it was possible to identify two small rooms of Royal Palace G, or, more precisely, of the "Audience Court," which served as archives for the storage of state documents. The first of these rooms (L. 2712) was found at the northern end of the east portico, and the second (L. 2769) toward the southern extremity of the same portico. Both rooms had been shaped under the high portico of the palace facade, raising thin partitions one brick thick, which supported light ceilings lower than the portico. The smaller of the two rooms (L. 2712), which has been completely excavated, was a storeroom. Here a limited number of tablets were arranged on high shelves . . . .

All this is very interesting, but obviously it is the report of an archaeologist rather than of an expert in ancient languages as such. He does actually touch on some literary aspects, as in his comment about the word "malikum" "king"; any Hebrew scholar will know that this is remarkably close to the Hebrew "malekh" (also meaning "king").

Matthiae also mentions that the word "AB. AB" can be translated "fathers," and again this is very close to the Hebrew term. He also tells us that gods such as Ishtar and Dagan seemed to be prominent, and of course these are the Ashtaroth and Dagon of the Bible—a Canaanite and Philistine goddess and god, respectively.

Professor Matthiae talks of the revolutionary nature of the finds at Ebla, and tells us, "the Ebla corpus would represent, even if no further texts should be found, one of the three major groups of documents in a Northwest Semitic language of antiquity, the other two being the Ugaritic texts and the Hebrew corpus of the Old Testament'' (p. 112).

He concludes his report with these words:

> Finally, it is the cultural reality of Early Syrian Ebla, with its predominance during the second half of the third millennium in Syria already evident, which must constitute the basis for all research that intends to study the culture traditionally defined as Canaanite, the culture in which one can recognize the ambience within which, in a complex process of influence and reaction, there occured the great religious experience of the Old Testament (p. 112).

Both the Italian Professors have made it clear that the whole of the research is still tenative, and a tremendous amount is yet to come. Both of them clearly are demonstrating the relevance of these Ebla finds to what Professor Matthiae has called ''the great religious experience of the Old Testament.''

One could wish that it was certain that no pressure had been brought on these two Italian Professors to minimize the relevance to Old Testament studies. However, with the delicate political situation between Syria and Israel, there is at least a doubt left in one's mind. Certain it is that Professor Freedman comes out of the issue as a man of integrity. He has done the world of scholarship a service by arranging for these two eminent Italian Professors to present their material to the English-speaking world, a job which they did very effectively.

MORE KITCHEN COMMENTS

Several other interesting points for the Bible student are made by Kenneth Kitchen in *The Bible In Its World* (InterVarsity Press, Illinois, our copy 1978). He refers to the collections of law found at Ebla, centuries older than those of Ur-Nammu of Ur or Hammurabi of Babylon. He suggests that the literary contribution will be very great. "Aided also by the rest of the archives, these special tablets will enable us to see the early history of many hundreds of words familiar from biblical Hebrew and its relatives such as Ugaritic and Phoenician" (p. 45).

He says as to the name Ya or Yaw, "If the form *Yaw* was actually an early form of YHWH, then of course the common misconception about Exodus 6:3, that the name YHWH was unknown before Moses, would be eliminated at a stroke, together with much of the 'critical' theories based in part upon such misconceptions" (p. 47). However, he suggests that there should be certain reservations until more definite information becomes available.

It is worth noting that Professor Buccellati confirmed the finding of the seal impression of Pepi I and also the cartouche of Cephren (sometimes called Khafre in translation), the cartouche being found on an alabaster bowl lid.

ANOTHER 20,000 TABLETS

It has been reported that a further 20,000 clay tablets have been found, but apparently these are not from the archive to which Professor Matthiae is referring. There seems to have been a veil of secrecy about the nature of the tablets, except to say that they are administrative texts. However, that is an all-inclusive term which could be used to minimize the importance of the new finds. Let it be said that the first tablets, eventually running into about 20,000, were also "administrative texts," but they have thrown a tremendous amount of light on the previously unknown empire centering out from Ebla. If there is the same amount of information from this further 20,000 "administrative texts," it will be satisfying indeed.

Unfortunately archaeological reports are notoriously slow in being presented in proper scholarly fashion, and it might be many years before we have a substantial flow of the many tablets already recovered. In addition, Ebla itself is a very large site, and it is likely that digging will proceed for many years yet.